ARCO
Literary Critiques

Jane Austen

Norman Sherry

36 22 13

arco
New York

To Sylvia

Acknowledgements

The portrait of Jane Austen on the cover and scenes from Bath are reproduced by permission of the Trustees of the British Museum. The illustration, 'Autumnal Walking Dress', from *The Novels of Jane Austen*, edited by R. W. Chapman, is reproduced by permission of the Oxford University Press, and the photograph of Chawton Cottage by permission of *The Times*.

Published 1969 by ARCO PUBLISHING COMPANY, Inc.
219 Park Avenue South, New York, N.Y. 10003
Copyright © Norman Sherry, 1966, 1969
All Rights Reserved
Library of Congress Catalog Number 71-78853
Printed in the United States of America

Arco Literary Critiques

Of recent years, the ordinary man who reads for pleasure has been gradually excluded from that great debate in which every intelligent reader of the classics takes part. There are two reasons for this: first, so much criticism floods from the world's presses that no one but a scholar living entirely among books can hope to read it all; and second, the critics and analysts, mostly academics, use a language that only their fellows in the same discipline can understand.

Consequently criticism, which should be as 'inevitable as breathing'—an activity for which we are all qualified—has become the private field of a few warring factions who shout their unintelligible battle cries to each other but make little communication to the common man.

Arco Literary Critiques aims at giving a straightforward account of literature and of writers—straightforward both in content and in language. Critical jargon is as far as possible avoided; any terms that must be used are explained simply; and the constant preoccupation of the authors of the Series is to be lucid.

It is our hope that each book will be easily understood, that it will adequately describe its subject without pretentiousness so that the intelligent reader who wants to know about Donne or Keats or Shakespeare will find enough in it to bring him up to date on critical estimates.

Even those who are well read, we believe, can benefit from a lucid exposition of what they may have taken for granted, and perhaps—dare it be said?—not fully understood.

K. H. G.

Jane Austen

In writing this book I had two aims in view. The first was to provide an introduction to Jane Austen which would be of use to those readers who were new to her work as well as to those who already know her novels but might not have found in them anything of particular importance or interest. Thus I hoped to inspire interest and understanding. My second aim was to give as balanced a picture of the novels as possible, keeping in mind recent revaluations of her works, without putting the emphasis too much upon one or other aspect of her art, so giving a distorted impression. In this I hoped to find appreciation from those who are already 'Janeites' and feel that a balanced writer deserves a balanced judgement.

Page numbers quoted throughout the text refer to the Chapman edition listed in the bibliography, but for the convenience of readers with other editions the chapters are numbered consecutively and not divided into volumes as in that work. The bibliography is intended only as a guide to the next stage of critical reading.

I am greatly indebted to the General Editor of the Series, Kenneth Grose, for his help at all stages of the manuscript. It was particularly welcome since I was so far from England during the writing and publication of the book.

N. S.

Contents

The Author

Norman Sherry, B.A., Ph.D., is lecturer in English Literature at the University of Singapore. He is author of *Conrad's Eastern World*.

Sydney Gardens, from New J.B. (....

Milsom Street, from Nattes' *Bath*, 1806

Chartwell Garden House

I

Her Life and Writings

'What is all this about Jane Austen? What is there *in* her? What is it all about?' asked Joseph Conrad of H. G. Wells. We do not know what Wells' reply was, but we can perhaps understand the puzzlement of the author of *Lord Jim* over such works as *Emma*. And, given the nature of her novels and their smallness in number, Jane Austen is a writer who arouses surprisingly strong reactions in her readers.

Her followers are perhaps the most fanatically attached that any author has had. Lord David Cecil said that those who do not like her are the kind of people who 'do not like sunshine or unselfishness'. During the Second World War she was extremely popular. Beatrice Kean Seymour wrote:

> In a society which has enthroned the machine-gun and carried it aloft even into the quiet heavens, there will always be men and women—Escapist or not, as you please—who will turn to her novels with an unending sense of relief and thankfulness.

And Winston Churchill tells us in *The Second World War*:

> I decided to read a novel. I had long ago read Jane Austen's *Sense and Sensibility*, and now I thought I would have *Pride and Prejudice.* . . . What calm lives they had, those people! No worries about the French Revolution, or the crashing struggle of the Napoleonic Wars. Only manners controlling natural passion so far as they could, together with cultured explanations of any mischances. All this seemed to go very well with M and B.   V, 377

On the other hand, Mark Twain said she inspired him with an 'animal repugnance', and Emerson said she was 'sterile' and 'vulgar'. Charlotte Brontë had no sympathy with her:

> She does her business of delineating the surface of the lives of genteel English people curiously well. . . . She ruffles her reader by nothing vehement, disturbs him by nothing profound. The passions are perfectly unknown to her; she rejects even a speaking acquaintance with that stormy sisterhood.

It is possible not to understand, or to misunderstand, the nature of Jane Austen's work, for her art is such that one can read only the surface and miss much of what exists underneath. The general impression is that her work reflects a calm, good-mannered, tranquil age, that it is comic and entertaining, that it is limited in its scope to polite society and in its range of emotions to those appropriate to young ladies within that society. And not all these impressions are mistaken. There is, however, a strong basis of moral seriousness to her work which must be taken into account for a full appreciation.

THE HISTORICAL BACKGROUND

It is wrong to conclude that Jane Austen lived during an uneventful period in history. Her short life (1775-1817) took place in the reign of George III and had several important events and changes as its background.

Primarily, it was the beginning of the transitional period between the eighteenth and nineteenth centuries, and saw the early growth of industrialisation. But the changes being brought about by factory life and the developing industrial revolution had not yet affected the life of country gentlemen in the south of England whose Great Houses provided the setting for seclusion and leisure, and whose wives had little to do but read poetry, gossip and sew. The Luddite riots, the reaction to industrialisation by machine-breaking which Charlotte Brontë wrote of in *Shirley*, did not take place till 1811-12. On the other hand, a new class of men was appearing who had made their money out of the new industries or in trade.

Religion gained strength through the Wesleyan movement which spread widely after 1791, and at the same time this was the period of greatest dandyism—the days of Beau Brummel.

In 1776, the States of America declared their independence, the French Revolution began in 1789, and from 1793 to 1815 England was involved in wars with France. It was the time of Nelson and Wellington, of Trafalgar (1805) and Waterloo (1815), and a consequent increase in importance of the army and navy.

These events are reflected in the novels to the extent that they must have been reflected in the lives of the people Jane Austen knew. They are not obtrusive, but they are present, and present particularly in the social changes they brought about.

Thus the militia and their camps have their part in the plot of *Pride and Prejudice*, and the navy as a career appears in *Mansfield Park* and *Persuasion*. Particularly in the latter novel, the navy is a means of improvement for men who are not rich and who can enrich themselves by promotion and prizes taken in battle. Sir Walter Elliot, in *Persuasion*, finds the navy offensive because it is 'the means of bringing persons of obscure birth into undue distinction' (*3*, 19). Admiral Croft can afford to rent Kellynch Hall. And Jane Austen, probably because two of her brothers were sailors, is obviously in sympathy with the energy, ideals, and comradeship of these men. She is aware of the sufferings of their families when the menfolk are long away, and of the results of disablement in battle (Captain Harville).

The importance of the colonies as a source of income is reflected in both *Persuasion* and *Mansfield Park*. The challenge of Methodism is referred to in the latter novel, and there is a passing notice of the slave trade in *Emma* from Mrs. Elton: '. . . if you mean a fling at the slave-trade, I assure you Mr. Suckling was always rather a friend to the abolition' (*35*, 300).

These are the vibrations caused by the impact of world events upon Jane Austen's life. It was a life in one respect less remarkable than those of her heroines, and in other respects less sheltered and undisturbed than her novels lead one to suppose. It was mainly the life of a country family, filled with the small duties and entertainments, the close relationships and warm attachments within the family circle that were typical of the times. While the excitements of romance, courtship, and marriage that form the patterns of her heroines' lives were not part of hers, she knew the anxieties of a sister who has two brothers in the navy during dangerous times, she was closely associated with a case of blackmail, and she may have been disappointed in love. Unlike her heroines, she was frequently in contact with death, for her father, several sisters-in-law and two close friends died within her short lifetime. And the troubles on the continent touched the Austen family when the husband of a cousin was guillotined during the French Revolution.

STEVENTON: 1775-1801

She was born on 16 December 1775 at the parsonage house of Steventon in Hampshire, where her father, the Reverend George Austen, was vicar. George Austen was a man of scholarship and prepared two of his sons for Oxford, but also occupied his time with his parish duties, his farm, and some pupils. Her mother, Cassandra Austen, was a countrywoman and a keen gardener.

They had six sons and two daughters. James, ten years older than Jane, became a minister and eventually succeeded his father at Steventon. The second son, George, is a mystery. Nothing is known of him except that Mrs. Austen said that 'poor little George' had fits. Edward, rather like Frank Churchill in *Emma*, was adopted by a rich relative, Thomas Knight of Godmersham Park in Kent and Chawton House in Hampshire, and became his heir. Henry Austen was in turn a militia officer, a banker, a bankrupt, and a curate—in that order. Henry was Jane's favourite brother, the handsomest of the family, with a bright and lovable nature, though it is possible that she is making fun of his style of letter-writing in Mr. Collins' letters in *Pride and Prejudice*. Henry wrote to the publisher about *Emma:*

> The politeness and perspicuity of your letter equally claim my earliest exertion. . . . Though I venture to differ occasionally from your critique, yet I assure you the quantum of your commendation rather exceeds than falls short of the author's expectation and my own.

And Mr. Collins wrote to Mr. Bennet:

As a clergyman, moreover, I feel it my duty to promote and establish the blessing of peace in all families within the reach of my influence; and on these grounds I flatter myself that my present overtures of good-will are highly commendable, and that the circumstance of my being next in the entail of Longbourn estate, will be kindly overlooked on your side, and not lead you to reject the offered olive branch.   PRIDE AND PREJUDICE *13*, 63

Preparing to hear Henry conduct the service at Chawton immediately after his Ordination, Jane wrote to a friend, 'It will be a nervous hour for our pew', and later to a nephew: 'Uncle Henry writes very superior Sermons'.

The other brothers, Francis and Charles, both became naval officers and eventually rose to the rank of admiral. Francis, in addition, received a knighthood.

Jane's one sister, Cassandra, was her close companion and friend. Her mother said that 'if Cassandra were going to have her head cut off, Jane would insist on sharing her fate'. Perhaps something of Cassandra's nature can be deduced from the fact that, of Jane's novels, *Mansfield Park* was her favourite. It was to Cassandra that many of Jane Austen's surviving letters were written when she and Cassandra were separated by visits to relatives or holidays away from home.

Within her immediate circle, therefore, were the kind of men we are accustomed to meet in the novels—a landowner, a militia officer, two clergymen, two sailors. And the circle was later widened by the addition of her brothers' wives (*five* of them married *nine* wives), and of their children, of whom there were a great number. Then there were neighbours and friends such as Mrs. Lefroy of Ashe, Martha Lloyd, and their cousins, Edward and Jane Cooper.

Steventon Vicarage was Jane Austen's home for twenty-five years, a house set in gentle, undramatic scenery—'tame country' her nephew described it—at the end of a small village of cottages, with the parish church on the hill nearby and further on the manor house, rented by the Digweed family. The Austen family's situation was similar to that of some of her heroines. They were at that time reasonably comfortably off, mixed in the best society of the neighbourhood, were hospitable, and kept a carriage and a pair of horses.

There is a family tradition that in 1782, when Jane was about seven, she and Cassandra were sent to be taught by a Mrs. Cawley, first at Oxford and then at Southampton, and that both girls fell ill of a putrid fever and that Jane almost died of it. Next the sisters went to the Abbey School at Reading, Jane being sent 'because she would have been miserable without her sister'. But by the time she was nine, Jane was back at home again and her formal education had come to an end. For their education after that the sisters must have depended largely upon their father and brothers, the cultured atmosphere of their home, and their contacts with relatives. Nor did this provide them with a poor education. Perhaps something of this is reflected in *Pride and Prejudice* when Elizabeth explains to Lady Catherine de Bourgh that she and her sisters had not the advantage of a governess but 'such of us as wished to learn, never wanted the means. We were always encouraged to read. . . .' (*29*, 165).

Jane Austen had read widely in certain fields, and reading played a substantial part in the life at Steventon Vicarage. This was reading not only to oneself, but aloud as a family entertainment, with all the discussions and criticisms it must have provoked. There are many references to such reading in her letters—'My father reads Cowper to us in the evening, to which I listen when I can'; 'Ought I to be very pleased with Marmion? —as yet I am not.—James reads it aloud in the Eveng—'. Poetry and drama made up part of the reading, and amateur theatricals were another leisure-time occupation of the family. Eliza de Feuillide, a cousin of the Austens and wife of the Comte de Feuillide who was later guillotined, took part in these theatricals. Another cousin wrote in 1787: 'They [Eliza and her mother] go at Christmas to Steventon and mean to act a play, *Which is the Man?* and *Bon Ton*. My uncle's barn is fitting up quite like a theatre, and all the young folks are to take their part.' No doubt Jane Austen was looking back to the family theatricals when she described the production of *Lover's Vows* in *Mansfield Park*.

Jane Austen had also the traditional accomplishments of the female of her day—she sang, played the piano, and drew. Dancing was an important form of amusement—it figures in most of her novels—and ranged from the extempore dances after a dinner party, to the monthly ball held in country towns in the winter. In September 1796, she wrote to Cassandra:

> *We* were at a Ball on Saturday I assure you. We dined at Goodnestone & in the Evening danced two Country Dances and the Boulangeries.—I opened the Ball with Edwd Bridges. . . . Elizth played one Country dance, Lady Bridges the other, which she made Henry dance with her. . . . On reading over the last three or four Lines, I am aware of my having expressed myself in so doubtful a manner that if I did not tell you to the contrary, You might imagine it was Lady Bridges who made Henry dance with her, at the same time that she was playing—which if not impossible must appear a very improbable Event to you.— But it was Eliz: who danced—.

Besides these accomplishments, Jane Austen read French and perhaps Italian, and was concerned with various domestic duties.

THE JUVENILIA

In such an environment it is little wonder that a girl of Jane Austen's talents began to write, and some of this early work survives in three notebooks entitled *Volume the First, Volume the Second* and *Volume the Third*. These volumes contain short novels, plays, scraps of writing, all done apparently before she was sixteen, and made unique by her own mistakes in spelling— 'freindship' and 'veiw' are generally mis-spelt—and by a strong comic spirit which shows itself in hilarious burlesques of the contemporary novel of horror and sentiment. *Love and Freindship* is particularly boisterous and, like the rest of the Juvenilia, obviously intended for family entertainment. The following extract shows her parodying the aspects of horror and sentimentality in contemporary novels:

> She had not time to answer me, for every thought was now engaged by the horrid Spectacle before us. Two Gentlemen most

elegantly attired but weltering in their blood was what first struck our Eyes—we approached—they were Edward and Augustus—. Yes dearest Marianne they were our Husbands. Sophia shreiked and fainted on the Ground—I screamed and instantly ran mad—. We remained thus mutually deprived of our Senses, some minutes, and on regaining them were deprived of them again. For an Hour and a Quarter did we continue in this unfortunate Situation—Sophia fainting every moment and I running Mad as often. LOVE AND FREINDSHIP *Letter the 13th*, 99

It is little wonder that the dying Sophia gives this advice to Laura:

Beware of fainting-fits. . . . Though at the time they may be refreshing and agreeable yet beleive me they will in the end, if too often repeated and at improper seasons, prove destructive to your Constitution. . . . My fate will teach you this. . . .
LOVE AND FREINDSHIP *Letter the 14th*, 102

By 1796 it is likely that a novel called *Elinor and Marianne*, written in the form of a series of letters, was completed, and this marked Jane Austen's movement from burlesque to more serious novels based on reality and dealing only with what was *probable* in real life. This was revised in 1797 and became *Sense and Sensibility*. From 1796 to 1797, when she was twenty-two, she was writing the first version of *Pride and Prejudice*, then called *First Impressions*, a title which gives us some idea of the theme she had in mind. And from 1797 to 1798 she was at work on *Susan*, the novel eventually to become *Northanger Abbey*. This was the first of her novels to be sold—sold but not published. It was bought by a publisher called Crosby in 1803, but it was never published by him.

First Impressions, however, was thought by her father to be good enough for publication, and he wrote offering it to a London publisher, Cadell, who does not seem to have been sufficiently interested to reply. The novel remained a favourite among the Austen family though, for in 1799 Jane wrote to Cassandra: 'I do not wonder at your wanting to read "First Impressions" again . . .' and in the same year: 'I would not let

Martha [Lloyd] read "First Impressions" again upon any account, and am very glad that I did not leave it in your power. She is very cunning, but I saw through her design; she means to publish it from memory, and one more perusal must enable her to do it.'

EVENTS AT STEVENTON

These works were written against a background of family travels, misfortunes and gaieties. Her letters at this time hint at a number of romances, or flirtations, but most often in jest: 'At length the day is come on which I am to flirt my last with Tom Lefroy, and when you receive this it will be over. My tears flow as I write at the melancholy idea.' However, there is a family tradition that, during a visit to Devonshire, she met a young man to whom she was much attracted, but that he died soon afterwards.

Cassandra also had her misfortunes, for in 1795 she became engaged to a young man who went out to the West Indies and died there from yellow fever in 1797. Eliza de Feuillide writes in a letter: 'Jane says that her sister behaves with a degree of resolution and propriety which no common mind could evince in so trying a situation.' And it was in 1794 that Eliza's husband had been guillotined.

In 1797, the Austens returned from a visit to Bath to learn that their brother Henry was engaged to be married to Eliza. Henry had given up the idea of becoming a clergyman and had joined the Oxford militia, and it has been suggested that it was Eliza's influence that made him alter his plans and give up the Ministry. This may be the origin of the conflict between Mary Crawford and Edmund Bertram in *Mansfield Park* over Edmund's ordination and Mary may have her origins in Eliza. And then in 1798 they learnt of the death of their friend Lady Williams, formerly Jane Cooper, in a chaise accident.

There was happier news in 1798, however, when Jane wrote jubilantly to her sister: 'Frank is made.—He was yesterday raised to the Rank of Commander & appointed to the Petterel Sloop, now at Gibraltar. . . . If you don't buy a muslin Gown now on the strength of . . . Frank's promotion, I shall never forgive you.' This reminds us of *Mansfield Park* and *Persuasion*, and we know that she asked her brother's permission, when she was writing the latter novel, to use the names of some of his ships for Captain Wentworth's commands.

In August of 1799, their father's sister, Mrs. Leigh Perrot, was accused at Bath of stealing a piece of lace. Untried prisoners had a hard lot in those days, and if by chance an unsympathetic jury had found her guilty she was liable to be transported. The situation was serious, and it seems that the accusation was a plot to force Mr. Perrot to pay money to have the charge withdrawn. Mrs. Perrot was in prison—or at least lodged in a house near to it—from August until the following March, waiting for the trial to come up. We know, from a letter written by Mrs. Perrot's cousin, that it was suggested that Jane or her sister should join her, though the offer was declined. Even though the event is not mentioned in any of Jane's extant letters, the family were obviously greatly concerned over it, and must have shared the relief of the Perrots when the jury returned a verdict of Not Guilty.

BATH AND SOUTHAMPTON: 1801-1809

In the spring of 1801 the Austens removed to Bath. Mr. Austen had reached retiring age, and Bath had been settled on as the place to which he would retire, perhaps because his brother-in-law, Mr. Leigh Perrot, spent several months of each year there. From this time the family income was reduced, and the need for economy became a constant concern.

It is said that Jane, then twenty-six—about the age of Anne Elliot in *Persuasion* when her family removed to Bath—was at first unhappy about living there. Perhaps she is expressing some of her own feeling when she writes of Anne: 'She disliked Bath, and did not think it agreed with her—and Bath was to be her home' (2, 14). But by January 1801 Jane seems to have got used to the idea for she writes to Cassandra:

> I get more & more reconciled to the idea of our removal. We have lived long enough in this Neighbourhood, the Basingstoke Balls are certainly on the decline, there is something interesting in the bustle of going away, & the prospect of spending future

summers by the Sea or in Wales is very delightful. . . . In what part of Bath do you mean to place your *Bees?*—We are afraid of the South Parade's being too hot.

And once in Bath she can write amusingly to Cassandra of the search for a house:

> When you arrive, we will at least have the pleasure of examining some of these putrifying Houses again;—they are so very desirable in size & situation, that there is some satisfaction in spending ten minutes within them.

—of the people she meets:

> I respect Mrs. Chamberlayne for doing her hair well, but cannot feel a more tender sentiment.—Miss Langley is like any other short girl with a broad nose & wide mouth, fashionable dress, & exposed bosom.

—and from Lyme of domestic matters:

> I endeavour as far as I can to supply your place & be useful, & keep things in order. I detect dirt in the water-decanter as fast as I can & give the Cook physic which she throws off her stomach. I forget whether she used to do this, under your administration.

—and of the conventions and amusements:

> Your unfortunate sister was betrayed last Thursday into a situation of the utmost cruelty. I arrived at Ashe Park before the Party from Deane, and was shut up in the drawing-room with Mr. Holder alone for ten minutes . . . . nothing could prevail on me to move two steps from the door, on the lock of which I kept one hand constantly fixed. We met nobody but ourselves, played at *vingt-un* again, and were very cross.

Her brothers in the navy continued to do well, and in 1801 she wrote to Cassandra:

> He [Charles] has received 30£ for his share of the privateer & expects 10£ more—but of what avail is it to take prizes if he lays out the produce in presents to his sisters. He has been buying gold chains & Topaze crosses for us;—he must be well scolded.

It will be remembered that Fanny Price's sailor brother, William in *Mansfield Park*, buys her an amber cross, and the finding of a gold chain for it involves Fanny in some embarrassments.

From Bath, the family went on expeditions to various places, one of them being Lyme Regis, the setting for part of *Persuasion*. And there is a family tradition that in 1802, while on a visit to James Austen at Steventon, Cassandra and Jane suddenly demanded one morning, without explanations, to be taken back to Bath immediately. Their haste and discomfiture were due to the fact that on the previous evening Jane had accepted a proposal of marriage, but the following morning decided that she could not marry simply from worldly motives, without love, and had changed her mind. If this is true, it shows a great deal of principle on her part, for she was later to write to her niece, Fanny Knight, 'Single Women have a dreadful propensity for being poor—which is one very strong argument in favour of Matrimony'.

During this period at Bath, her mother was for some time seriously ill, and her father and her friend Mrs. Lefroy died within a month of each other in 1804–5. It was not a happy period for her, and she wrote later: 'It will be two years tomorrow since we left Bath for Clifton, with what happy feelings of Escape!'.

Perhaps because of this, Jane Austen does not appear to have written very much at this time. *Susan* was completed and a novel called *The Watsons* was begun, but this remained unfinished even at her death.

In 1806 they finally left Bath for Clifton, and in the autumn they settled in lodgings in Southampton.

CHAWTON: 1809-1817

In October 1808, Elizabeth Austen, wife of Edward, the brother who had been adopted by the Knights, died very suddenly. And wanting to 'bind his mother and sisters more closely to himself', Edward offered them a choice of homes—they could have either a house near his estate at Godmersham, or Chawton Cottage near his other home, Chawton House, in Hampshire. By July 1809 they were in their new home, Chawton Cottage.

It is interesting to note Jane's renewed interest in her writing at this point, for before leaving Southampton she wrote to Crosby, the publisher who had bought *Susan* in 1803, inquiring about its publication, and received the reply that she could buy back the manuscript for ten pounds.

Chawton Cottage was 'so close to the road that the front door opened upon it', but Edward blocked up the large drawing-room window which overlooked the road and opened another 'at the side which gave to view only turf and trees'. It had a good-sized entrance and two sitting-rooms made the length of the house 'and was capable of receiving other members of the family as frequent visitors'. At Chawton, Mrs. Austen, Cassandra, Jane, and Martha Lloyd who then lived with them, returned to the quiet life of the country, enlivened by visits from the family and to the family. It was in this house that Jane Austen spent the remaining eight years of her life.

The move to Chawton led to a new spate of writing, and for the first time she began to publish. It is surprising that her life as a publishing author lasted only six years. She was a careful reviser of her work, and the writing of a novel often stretched over a long period. *Sense and Sensibility* would appear to be a complete re-writing of the earlier *Elinor & Marianne* and a re-casting of it from letter-form into third person narrative. Much of this revision must have been carried out at Chawton, and *Sense and Sensibility* was the first of her novels to be published, appearing in the autumn of 1811 when Jane Austen was thirty-six, after an apprenticeship to writing that had begun when she was twelve. From now onwards references to her novels and their characters become frequent in her letters, and in 1813 she writes to Francis Austen, one of the naval brothers: 'You will be glad to hear that every Copy of S. & S. is sold & that it has brought me £140'.

The following years were fruitful ones for her. *Pride and Prejudice*, the revised form of *First Impressions*, appeared in January 1813, and Jane writes to Cassandra: 'I want to tell you that I have got my own darling child from London; on Wednesday I received one copy sent down by Falknor.... I must confess that I think her [Elizabeth Bennet] as delightful a creature as ever appeared in print. . . . ' *Mansfield Park*, which had been begun in 1811, was published in 1814, and *Emma*, begun in 1814, appeared in 1815. She had permission to dedicate this novel to the Prince Regent.

Perhaps as a result of the success of *Emma*, her brother Henry bought back the manuscript of *Susan* from Crosby the publisher for ten pounds, and revision must have begun on this also—it was to become *Northanger Abbey*. In 1815 *Persuasion* was begun and in 1817 she writes to Fanny Knight, 'You may *perhaps* like the Heroine, as she is almost too good for me'.

We know from her nephew how her creative work was done:

> . . . she had no separate study to retire to, and most of the work must have been done in the general sitting-room, subject to all kind of casual interruptions. She was careful that her occupation should not be suspected by servants, or visitors, or any persons beyond her own family party. She wrote upon small sheets of paper which could easily be put away, or covered with a piece of blotting paper. There was, between the front door and the offices, a swing door which creaked when it was opened; but she objected to having this little inconvenience remedied, because it gave her notice when anyone was coming.

Jane Austen wished to remain anonymous, and it was not until after the publication of *Pride and Prejudice* that the secret of her authorship was given away by her brother Henry. She tried to laugh away her discomfiture at being discovered: 'I do not despair of having my picture in the Exhibition at last—all white & red, with my Head on one Side. . . .' Even then she remained in retirement, never taking part in the literary world of her day.

Until 1816, when she was forty, there was no sign of Jane Austen being ill, but early in that year some friends whom she visited 'thought that her health was somewhat impaired, and observed that she went about her old haunts, and recalled old recollections connected with them in a particular manner, as if she did not expect ever to see them again'. She still wrote cheerful letters to her relatives, but she became less and less active. Perhaps an effect of her illness is reflected in a reference to *Northanger Abbey* in 1817: 'Miss Catherine is put upon the Shelve for the present, and I do not know that she will ever come out. . . .' However, this novel and *Persuasion* were finished, and a final novel, *Sanditon*, begun.

In 1817 she wrote to her friend, Miss Bigg: '*I* have certainly gained strength through the winter and am not far from being well'. But in the spring of that year her niece visited her and later recalled: 'I was struck by the alteration in herself. . . . She was not equal to the exertion of talking to us, and our visit to the sick room was a very short one'.

In May, she and Cassandra went to Winchester to get further medical advice, but there was no hope of a cure. They took lodgings in College Street, and from there Jane wrote to a nephew: 'I will not boast of my handwriting; neither that nor my face have yet recovered their proper beauty, but in other respects I am gaining strength very fast.' And to a friend, Anne Sharp: 'I can sit up in my bed & employ myself. . . . I am now really a very genteel, portable sort of an Invalid.' In spite of the cheerful tone of such letters, she was seriously ill, and she died on 18 July 1817, aged only forty-one. She was buried in Winchester Cathedral. Cassandra wrote afterwards to Fanny Knight:

> I *have* lost a treasure, such a sister, such a friend as never can have been surpassed. She was the sun of my life, the gilder of every pleasure, the soother of every sorrow; I had not a thought concealed from her, and it is as if I had lost a part of myself.

HER APPEARANCE AND CHARACTER

Several reports of Jane Austen's appearance and character have come down to us from her contemporaries—not all of them complimentary, and not all reliable.

In 1788, when Jane was twelve, she and Cassandra visited their great-uncle at Sevenoaks, and met their cousin Philadelphia Walter. Philadelphia wrote of them:

> Yesterday I began an acquaintance with my two female cousins, Austens. . . . The youngest [Jane] is very like her brother Henry, not at all pretty and very prim, unlike a girl of twelve. . . .

And a day or two later:

> Yesterday they all spent the day with us, and the more I see of Cassandra the more I admire [her]. Jane is whimsical and affected.

Mrs. Lefroy's brother, however, who rented Mr. Austen's Parsonage at Deane in 1788, recorded:

> When I knew Jane Austen I never suspected that she was an authoress; but my eyes told me that she was fair and handsome, slight and elegant, but with cheeks a little too full.

And Eliza de Feuillide, in 1792, gives a pleasanter picture:

> . . . Cassandra and Jane are both very much grown (the latter is now taller than myself), and greatly improved as well in manners as in person. . . . They are I think equally sensible and both so to a degree seldom met with, but still my heart gives the preference to Jane, whose kind partiality to me indeed requires a return of the same nature.

Less complimentary are the comments of the novelist Mary Russell Mitford. Writing in 1815, she recalled that her mother remembered Jane Austen as 'the prettiest, silliest, most affected husband-hunting butterfly'. But Mrs. Mitford's memory must have failed her—Jane Austen was only eight when Mrs. Mitford knew her. Mary Mitford goes on, however:

> . . . she has stiffened into the most perpendicular, precise, taciturn piece of 'single blessedness' that ever existed, and . . . till 'Pride and Prejudice' showed what a precious gem was hidden in that unbending case, she was no more regarded in society than a poker or a fire screen or any other thin, upright piece of wood or iron that fills its corner in peace and quiet. The case is very different now; she is still a poker, but a poker of whom everyone is afraid. It must be confessed that this silent observation from such an observer is rather formidable . . . a wit, a delineator of character who does not talk is formidable indeed.

Certainly this does not sound like the creator of Elizabeth Bennet and Emma Woodhouse, and there is something malicious in the sound of it. It seems likely that Jane, moving as she did within a close family circle and not a boisterous person when in company, would be little known, intimately, outside the family. And the reports of her family—though probably too partial—give a different impression. Her nephew wrote:

> In person she was very attractive; her figure was rather tall and slender, her step light and firm, and her whole appearance expressive of health and animation. In complexion she was a clear brunette with a rich colour; she had full round cheeks, with mouth and nose small and well formed, bright hazel eyes, and brown hair forming natural curls close round her face.

And her nieces recalled how 'Her first charm to children was great sweetness of manner. She seemed to love you, and you loved her in return . . . she would tell us the most delightful stories, chiefly of Fairyland.' Her niece Anna adds—what was probably responsible for the wrong impression the novelist gave to those who did not know her well—that 'She was in fact one of the last people in society to be afraid of. I do not suppose she ever in her life said a sharp thing. She was naturally shy and not given to talk much in company, and people fancied, knowing that she was clever, that she was on the watch for good material for books.' She was not only shy, she was also at times very grave, but she could be merry enough with her friends.

In none of these reports do we find the ironical, and sometimes malicious, but always humorous, Jane of the letters and novels, and the real Jane Austen must lie somewhere between the 'taciturn piece of single-blessedness' and the virtuous sister and aunt. It is in the letters that we find the qualities of mind responsible for the novels—a quickness of observation, a sense of the incongruous, and an awareness of the comedy of society:

> Miss Fletcher and I were very thick, but I am the thinnest of the two—She wore her purple Muslin, which is pretty enough, tho' it does not become her complexion.

> Mr. Richard Harvey is going to be married; but as it is a great secret, & only known to half the Neighbourhood, you must not mention it.

2

The Literary Background

Her life, her quality of mind, and finally her reading—the third important influence for her writing. What was the literary background against which Jane Austen's novels can be set and from which they developed?

Living as she did between 1775 and 1817, her life spans an important period in English literary history. She stood between the eighteenth and nineteenth centuries, between what we might describe as the Age of Reason and the Age of Romanticism—the Age of Sense and the Age of Sensibility.

Speaking very generally, we can say that the eighteenth century had been a period which appreciated a reasonable, urbane attitude to life. Behind the writer was the belief that there was a 'right way' for the universe to work, that there was a permanent 'truth' of human behaviour, and that reason should govern all things. Uncontrolled emotion was not approved of. Order, reason, propriety, awareness of traditions, were the goals in life and literature. Prose of the moral kind of Dr. Johnson, the *Spectator* and the *Tatler*, and the well-balanced, witty couplets of Pope's verse were the typical literary forms.

Towards the end of the century, however, other attitudes gained strength which were to change the outlook of the English people. The Romantic movement in literature and the Methodist movement in religion were aspects of this new outlook, as was the development of landscape painting in art. Generally speaking, the individual's own instinct and feeling began to be recognised as the basis for judgement, as having its own relevancy and rightness, rather than some general and accepted reasonable code. The individual's response to life, and necessarily his *emotional* response, was the important thing.

There was, of course, no abrupt change from one outlook to the other. The transition was gradual and never final, though we can see its beginnings in literature as early as Cowper and Thomson, and it was first established with the issuing of Blake's *Songs of Innocence* in 1789 and Wordsworth's *Lyrical Ballads* in 1798. The poetry of Burns was another aspect of this movement in literature, as were Scott's long, narrative and romantic poems with their historical themes (his novels began appearing only towards the end of Jane Austen's life).

The conflict between the two attitudes of mind, which was felt most strongly about this time, is summarised—humorously —by Mr. Crotchet in Thomas Love Peacock's novel, *Crotchet Castle* (1831):

> 'The sentimental against the rational, the intuitive against the inductive, the ornamental against the useful, the intense against the tranquil, the romantic against the classical; these are great and interesting controversies, which I should like, before I die, to see satisfactorily settled.'

SENSE AND SENSIBILITY

The danger of the new emphasis upon emotion was, of course, that undisciplined emotion could lead to states of mind that were not healthy, and actions that were not wise. And the fashionable emphasis upon feeling and upon displays of emotion might lead to hypocrisy—the pretending to an emotion that was not really felt.

Dr. Johnson hated 'feelers'—that is, those who developed and demonstrated their emotional response to the world, their sensibility. But Johnson as an eighteenth-century man could approve of a 'natural' response as being according to man's nature, the controlling force of which is reason, not emotion. To him, anything beyond this became suspect. And as the cult of sensibility developed, the display of emotion for its own sake became too common. Consider the extravagance (satirical, perhaps) of Laurence Sterne's apostrophe to 'Sensibility' in *A Sentimental Journey:*

Dear Sensibility! source inexhausted of all that's precious in our joys, or costly in our sorrows! . . . Eternal fountain of our feelings! . . . I feel some generous joys and generous cares beyond myself;—all comes from thee, great,—great *Sensorium* of the world!

We are approaching the conflict which appears in greater or lesser degree in all Jane Austen's novels, from the Juvenilia onwards. The idea of Sensibility, of strong emotional reaction to every aspect of life, was opposed to the earlier recommendation of Sense, which implies restraint of the emotions and imagination and reliance on reason. The cult of Sensibility was to lead to exaggeration and affectation, but it also brought about a greater concern for the predicament of the poor and sick, the awareness of the special life of childhood, an appreciation of the wilder beauties of nature, an interest in past history, in the workings of the imagination and in the supernatural. The two opposing qualities are clearly portrayed in Jane Austen's novel, *Sense and Sensibility:*

> Marianne's abilities were, in many respects, quite equal to Elinor's. She was sensible and clever; but eager in every thing: her sorrows, her joys, could have no moderation. She was generous, amiable, interesting: she was every thing but prudent. . . .
>
> Elinor saw, with concern, the excess of her sister's sensibility but by Mrs. Dashwood it was valued and cherished. They encouraged each other now in the violence of their affliction. The agony of grief which overpowered them at first, was voluntarily renewed, was sought for, was created again and again . . . Elinor, too, was deeply afflicted; but still she could struggle, she could exert herself.   *i*, 6-7.

And Edward Ferrars, in comparing his own opinion of Barton with Marianne's, contrasts the eighteenth- and the nineteenth-century outlook—the Classical and the Romantic:

> 'I call it very fine country—the hills are steep, the woods seem full of fine timber, and the valley looks comfortable and snug—with rich meadows and several neat farm houses scattered here and there. It exactly answers my idea of a fine country, because

it unites beauty with utility—and I dare say it is a picturesque one too, because you admire it; I can easily believe it to be full of rocks and promontories, grey moss and brush wood. . . .' *18*, 97

Sense admires orderliness and utility, the prominent and striking features, the civilised landscape to which one can give a reasoned approval; Sensibility admires irregularity, wildness, and grandeur, the minute and the particular, to which one responds intuitively and emotionally.

THE NOVEL

The novel also was affected by this change of outlook. The eighteenth century had been the great period for the development of the novel into the form of literature with which we are familiar today. That is to say that the idea of plot, of psychological insight into character, and of the presentation of the story against what can be called a 'realistic' setting, had all been developed by the time Jane Austen began to write.

Her three most important predecessors were Samuel Richardson whose first novel, *Pamela*, was published in 1740; Henry Fielding who published *Joseph Andrews* in 1742; and Fanny Burney, who published *Evelina* in 1778.

Richardson's novel told the story of a virtuous heroine in the power of a seducer determined to overcome her virtue. Pamela, daughter of poor parents, held out and eventually married her persecutor, a rich landowner. Hence the sub-title of the story, *Virtue Rewarded*. In his second novel, *Clarissa*, the heroine is less fortunate, but in all Richardson's novels the emphasis is upon psychological insight and analysis of motive and character, and the appreciation of emotion for its own sake. They are tales of constant tension, unclouded virtue and unbelievable villainy. Especially he is important for showing characters who think, feel and act without the intrusion of comment from the author.

Henry Fielding wrote his first novel in reaction to Richardson's *Pamela*. *Joseph Andrews* was intended as a satire on Richardson's novel, but became a novel in its own right. In this and in *Tom Jones* (1749), Fielding is a satirical and comic writer who uses exaggeration for his comic ends, a portrayer of society, boisterous, licentious, with a strong vein of irony, and an ability at dialogue that must surely have influenced Jane Austen.

Fielding's characters, especially his women, are seen from the male point of view. In contrast, *Evelina* deals with a young girl's entry into the society of London and Bath, and it is a novel seen from her point of view, with a woman's understanding and observation. Evelina encounters misunderstandings and embarrassments through her own inexperience, and meets a great variety of characters during her adventures. She, perhaps, is too good to be true, too innocent, too beautiful, but the novel mirrors the manners of the age, conversations, pastimes, people and their characteristics very convincingly. Fanny Burney's portraits of a certain class are very vivid—she makes use of the slips of syntax and pronunciation which reveal the ill-educated, the remarks that reveal the vulgar mind, and Jane Austen was to take this up later with such characters as the Misses Steele in *Sense and Sensibility*.

It was from such novelists that Jane Austen could learn her art, but she developed it in her own way. Her change of emphasis was in limiting herself to what she personally knew of life, of bringing vice and virtue within the bounds of what was likely in a society of ordinary people and their moral code, and of generally sticking close to the laws of probability. It is interesting that while forcible seductions or attempts at seduction form part of other novels, they are never part of hers. Seduction is replaced by elopement, a more likely occurrence, and requiring the consent of the lady involved.

THE GOTHIC NOVEL AND THE NOVEL OF SENTIMENT

Jane Austen was writing at a time when the novel was extremely popular, and when, since books were expensive, circulating libraries became the source from which they were obtained. There, the reader could borrow the three-volume novels for a charge which might be as much as 2d. a day for each volume.

The most popular kind of novel of the time circulated by the libraries was the Gothic or horror novel, the first of these being Horace Walpole's *Castle of Otranto* (1764).

The plot of such novels usually involved an amazingly virtuous and beautiful heroine in all kinds of terrifying adventures, generally in a foreign land—Italy was popular because of the *banditti*. Murders, sadistic villains, old, ruinous, haunted buildings, long-lost children, explanatory documents hidden in secret drawers—all that could shock and horrify the reader were part of the trappings of these novels. There were other conventions—the heroine was usually loved by an equally virtuous hero to whom she was eventually united, and there was usually some mystery about her birth or his.

Popular at the same time were the novels of sentiment, which drew on many of the conventions of the Gothic novel, though the emphasis was upon emotional and pathetic situations rather than upon those of horror and suspense, the characters displaying a strong sensibility. Jane Austen's burlesque of these novels, quoted in the previous chapter, can be seen to be not so great an exaggeration of the style of the novel of sentiment when we compare it with this passage from Henry Mackenzie's *The Man of Feeling* (1771). The passage describes the hero's reaction to having his proposal of marriage accepted:

> He seized her hand—a languid colour reddened his cheek—a smile brightened faintly in his eye. As he gazed on her, it grew dim, it fixed, it closed. He sighed and fell back on his seat—Miss Walton screamed at the sight. His aunt and the servants rushed into the room. They found them lying motionless together. His physician happened to call at that instant. Every art was tried to recover them; with Miss Walton they succeeded—but Harley was gone forever!

Evelina is built upon many of the conventions of the novel of sentiment in spite of its realistic presentation. Take the heroine's meeting with her father, whom she has never seen before:

> Then, taking my trembling hand, she led me forward. I would have withdrawn it, and retreated, but as he advanced instantly towards me, I found myself already before him.
>
> What a moment for your Evelina!—an involuntary scream escaped me, and covering my face with my hands, I sunk on the floor.

He had, however, seen me first; for in a voice scarce articulate, he exclaimed, 'My God! does Caroline Evelyn [Evelina's dead mother] still live!' . . . .

Affected beyond measure, I half arose, and embraced his knees, while yet on my own.

In Jane Austen's *Love and Freindship*, we have the discovery not of a long-lost *father*, but of a long-lost *grandfather*:

> At his first Appearance my Sensibility was wonderfully affected and e'er I had gazed at him a 2^d time, an instinctive sympathy whispered to my Heart, that he was my Grandfather . . . I threw myself on my knees before him and besought him to acknowledge me as his Grand Child. . . . 'I do acknowledge thee. . . .' While he was thus tenderly embracing me, Sophia . . . entered the Room in search of me . . . he [the Grandfather] exclaimed . . . 'Another Granddaughter! . . .' LOVE AND FREINDSHIP *Letter the 11th*, 91

And when several more grandchildren have appeared:

> 'But tell me (continued he looking fearfully towards the Door) tell me, have I any other Grand-children in the House.' 'None my Lord.' 'Then I will provide for you all without farther delay—Here are 4 Banknotes of 50£ each—Take them and remember I have done the Duty of a Grandfather.' He instantly left the Room and immediately afterwards the House.
>
> LOVE AND FREINDSHIP *Letter the 11th*, 92

JANE AUSTEN'S READING

Jane Austen's reading extended over the reasoned, and reasonable, the witty, and the moral literature of the eighteenth century—Johnson, Pope, and Crabbe; through the beginnings of romanticism in Cowper and Thomson; over its romantic, historical aspects in Scott's poems; and its extravagances of emotion in the sentimental and Gothic novels.

She was, according to her nephew, 'well acquainted with the old periodicals from the "Spectator" downwards', and she knew very well the novels of Richardson, Sterne, Fielding, Fanny Burney. 'Amongst her favourite writers, Johnson in prose, Crabbe in verse, and Cowper in both, stood high.' 'Scott's poetry gave her great pleasure.' In history she 'followed the old guides—Goldsmith, Hume, and Robertson'. Her own copies, bearing her signature, of Hume's *History*, Thomson's *Works*, Goldsmith's *Animated Nature*, Hayley's *Poems and Plays*, have been recovered. The poetry of Pope, Gray and Byron was known to her, and she had read various works on the 'picturesque' in landscape and landscape gardening.

References to her reading appear in many of her novels. Henry Crawford in *Mansfield Park* reads Shakespeare. Marianne Dashwood's favourite topics for discourse were the beauties of Cowper and Scott, the limitations of Pope, second marriages and picturesque beauty. Anne Elliot, talking to the melancholy Captain Benfield at Lyme, tried 'to ascertain whether *Marmion* or *The Lady of the Lake* were to be preferred, and how ranked the *Giaour* and *The Bride of Abydos;* and, moreover, how the *Giaour* was to be pronounced' (*P. 10,* 100). And Anne, eighteenth-century in her attitude to sensibility, ventures to say that 'she thought it was the misfortune of poetry, to be seldom safely enjoyed by those who enjoyed it completely; and . . . she ventured to recommend a larger allowance of prose in his daily study . . . our best moralists . . . collections of the finest letters. . . .' (*P. 10,* 101). In *Northanger Abbey*, Catherine is reading Mrs. Radcliffe's famous horror novel, *The Mysteries of Udolpho*, and is given a list of further novels by Isabella, who assures her that they are all 'horrid': '*Castle of Wolfenbach, Clermont, Mysterious Warnings, Necromancer of the Black Forest, Midnight Bell, Orphan of the Rhine,* and *Horrid Mysteries*' (*6,* 40).

INFLUENCE OF CONTEMPORARY FICTION

Jane Austen was, therefore, well acquainted with the literature and the literary movements of her time, and their influence is an all-pervasive one in her works. She is of the eighteenth century in her moral outlook, and in her prose style, but she is fully aware of the new strains of romanticism. Her work begins as a reaction to the contemporary popular novel—indeed, *Northanger Abbey* cannot be fully appreciated without some acquaintance with *The Mysteries of Udolpho, The Romance of the Forest, Emmeline, the Orphan of the Castle,* and *Evelina*.

33

Jane Austen's *comic* 'Plan of a Novel' reveals her awareness of those fields of sentimentality and 'Gothicness' that were not for her. This Plan, drawn up 'according to hints from various quarters', is published with her Juvenilia:

> Scene to be in the Country, Heroine the Daughter of a Clergyman. . . . He, the most excellent Man that can be imagined, perfect in Character, Temper & Manners . . . Heroine a faultless Character herself—, perfectly good, with much tenderness & sentiment, & not the least Wit . . . Her Person, quite beautiful . . . From this outset, the Story will proceed, & contain a striking variety of adventures. Heroine & her Father never above a fortnight together in one place, *he* being driven from his Curacy by the vile arts of some totally unprincipled & heart-less young Man, desperately in love with the Heroine, & pursuing her with unrelenting passion . . . but all the Good will be unexceptionable in every respect—and there will be no foibles or weaknesses but with the Wicked, who will be completely depraved and infamous. . . .
> 428-429

Jane Austen would have said, like Virginia Woolf, that 'life is very far from being "like this"', and so her novels deal with what for her, and within certain fictional conventions, life *was* like.

The contrast in Jane Austen's mind between the fanciful adventures and sentimental vapourings of the average novel and the prosaicness of the actual world established itself early, and never left her work. It provided her with a means of wit, humour and irony. But at the same time, she was fully aware of the incongruities in actual life—the incongruities of behaviour, the difference between the affected and the actual feelings of the people she met. And to her mind, these were of greater interest than any imagined adventures.

As a result, we have the kind of realistic, ironically humorous, social comedy which does not depend upon sentimental effects or extraordinary dangers to hold the interest of the reader, which does not require descriptions of magnificent and foreign scenery, of storms, ancient castles, brigands and villains, or, alternatively, pathetic incidents, or even a Mr. Rochester, that middle-class hero-villain of Charlotte Brontë's *Jane Eyre*.

3

Her Limitations and Strengths

No one would deny that as a novelist Jane Austen works within strict limitations. This is often put forward as a criticism of her work. It has been said, for example, that she had only one plot. And the Cockney mess-waiter in Kipling's story *The Janeites* is simply expressing this view when he says of her novels:

> ' 'Twasn't as if there was anythin' *to* 'em either. *I* know. I had to read 'em. They weren't adventurous, nor smutty, nor what you'd call even interestin'—all about girls o' seventeen (they begun young then, I tell you), not certain 'oom they'd like to marry; an' their dances an' card-parties an' picnics, and their young blokes goin' off to London on 'orseback for 'air-cuts an' shaves.'

The implication is that her subject matter is limited, superficial, repetitive, and without any real seriousness or relevance to life.

Certain limitations were imposed upon her by the conventions of the romantic novel, whose plot demanded that she should deal with the courtship and marriage of her heroine. We will consider this aspect in a later chapter. But she herself claimed that she worked on a 'little bit (two Inches wide) of Ivory'. She was conscious of her limitations, worked strictly within them, and turned them to her advantage.

THE LIMITATIONS OF EXPERIENCE

The area of experience with which she could deal was naturally determined by her own life. She has been said to hold a mirror up to life and it is apparent to any reader of her letters that she mirrors the life she knew. The family names—Marianne, Anne, Henry; the family professions—the church, the militia, the navy, land-owning; the family gatherings, journeys, walks; the countryside she knew; the streets of Bath and Lyme; the conventions and the manners of her time are all recorded. But we must remember that the mirror is not a true one—it is deflected by her own outlook as moralist and ironist.

Her interest is in human motive, the reactions of individuals to each other, and therefore a narrow social setting was ideal material for her. The small area of experience allowed closer analysis of recurring situations and types; she could deal with them with absolute accuracy by never stepping beyond the limits of her personal knowledge.

A narrow physical setting—a country town, a country house, Bath; a narrow social setting—the three or four families within such a society who would be on visiting terms; a narrow moral setting—the manners and morals accepted within that society; a narrow character range—most of the characters being middle-class; a limited plot—the range of events likely to occur within that setting; these are the limitations of her art, and at the same time the discipline of her art.

ACCURACY AND REALISM

Not only was she aware of the limitations of her experience, but she refused to be tempted beyond them. Her advice to her niece Anna, who had also taken to novel-writing, was to prevent her moving with certain characters out of England:

> And we think you had better not leave England. Let the Portmans go to Ireland, but as you know nothing of the Manners there, you had better not go with them. You will be in danger of giving false representations. Stick to Bath & the Foresters. There you will be quite at home.

Jane Austen always 'stuck to' Bath, Lyme Regis, a country house, or a country village—the places she knew and the people she knew to inhabit them. And she never tried to show them through a viewpoint other than her own. Thus, we never see men except in the presence of women. What they got up to out of the drawing-room and female society we don't know. Perhaps we should say *virtuous* female society. We learn of their behaviour with the less virtuous of the sex only by hearsay! But certainly, we never see the gentlemen shaving, hunting, playing billiards, gambling, or attending to business. No doubt these were fields beyond her experience.

But within that experience she had what was almost an obsession for accuracy as to the facts, and as to the probability of events within that environment. While writing *Mansfield Park* she was anxious to find out whether there were hedgerows in Northamptonshire, the county in which the novel is set. A 'hedgerow' in this sense is 'an irregular border of copse-wood and timber, often wide enough to contain within it a winding footpath, or a rough cart-track'. Readers of *Persuasion* will remember how useful a hedgerow is for Anne to overhear the conversation between Captain Wentworth and Louisa Musgrove. But *Persuasion* was set in Somerset where such hedgerows existed. They were not to be found in Northamptonshire and therefore do not figure in *Mansfield Park*.

She was concerned even with *probable* topics of conversation and interest within a certain geographical area. On this point she wrote to her niece Anna pointing out a mistake Anna had made: 'Lyme will not do. Lyme is towards 40 miles distance from Dawlish & would not be talked of there.—I have put Starcross instead.' And in the same letter, she makes a further correction of Anna's manuscript with reference to correctness of social intercourse: 'I have also scratched out the Introduction between Lord P. & his brother, & Mr. Griffin. A Country Surgeon . . . would not be introduced to Men of their rank.'

One can always be sure that her characters will take the correct time over a journey, and go by the correct route. She constructed her novels wth the almanac of a particular year in mind so that the passage of time also is plotted. She *did* make a mistake in *Emma* in having orchards in blossom at the same time as her characters were picking strawberries at Donwell Abbey! But generally, she is so accurate that her theatres and concerts, Upper Rooms and Lower Rooms at Bath are always on the right days of the week.

Perhaps because of this concern to limit herself to what she knew and to reflect it accurately, the world she portrays has a great feeling of reality and convincingness. That she herself felt the reality of her characters is shown by her willingness to discuss with her family what happened to her characters after the novels had ended:

> We have been both to the Exhibition & Sir J. Reynolds',—and I am disappointed, for there was nothing like Mrs. D[arcy] at either. I can only imagine that Mr. D. prizes any Picture of her too much to like it should be exposed to the public eye.

And her family learnt that Miss Steele never succeeded in catching the Doctor; that Kitty Bennet was satisfactorily married to a clergyman near Pemberley; and that the letters placed by Frank Churchill before Jane Fairfax, which she swept away unread, formed the word 'Pardon'.

The convincingness of her novels is reflected in Tennyson's request on arriving at Lyme Regis: 'Now take me to the Cobb, and show me the steps where Louisa Musgrove fell.'

THE SOCIAL SETTING

Each novel has, then, a firm social setting. The opening of each reveals this immediately. *Northanger Abbey* begins with the heroine's name, and goes on to outline her family's social and monetary status exactly:

> Her father was a clergyman, without being neglected, or poor, and a very respectable man. . . . He had a considerable independence, besides two good livings . . . (*1*, 13). Mr. Allen, who owned the chief of the property about Fullerton, the village in Wiltshire where the Morlands lived . . . (*1*, 17).

Persuasion begins, not with the heroine, but with her father, who is also firmly placed: 'Sir Walter Elliot, of Kellynch-hall, in Somersetshire, was a man who, for his own amusement, never took up any book but the Baronetage . . .' (*1*, 3). And from the Baronetage we are given full details of the family and its connections. *Mansfield Park* opens with Miss Maria Ward, of

Huntingdon, with only seven thousand pounds, who 'had the good luck to captivate Sir Thomas Bertram, of Mansfield Park, in the county of Northampton, and to be thereby raised to the rank of a baronet's lady. . .' (*1*, 3). The beginning of *Sense and Sensibility* tells us that 'The family of Dashwood had been long settled in Sussex. Their estate was large, and their residence was at Norland Park. . .' (*1*, 3). Emma is also quickly placed—'handsome, clever, and rich'—though the social setting is established rather later: 'Highbury, the large and populous village almost amounting to a town, to which Hartfield, in spite of its separate lawn and shrubberies and name, did really belong. . .' (*1*, 7). But very early in *Pride and Prejudice* we learn that 'Netherfield is taken by a young man of large fortune from the north of England. . .' (*1*, 3). And each novel has its Great House, its vicarage, its small town or village, and the narrow range of inhabitants on visiting terms with the Great House.

It is from this restricted social setting, this sense of accuracy and precision of portrayal, that in large part comes the feeling of security and order, the atmosphere of calmness and deliberation, for which many people read Jane Austen. Nothing terrible can happen in such a setting, and indeed nothing terrible ever does. The greatest harm that can occur is veiled by good manners; and an unpleasant character—a Mrs. Norris—does not ultimately affect the outcome of the story for the heroine. Almost all the action takes place through the dialogue—a mannered, socially approved dialogue. Anything really unpleasant—a duel, an elopement, a death—takes place off-stage. 'Only manners controlling natural passion so far as they could, together with cultured explanations of any mischances', as Sir Winston Churchill said.

Is there any more to her novels than this? Are we, for example, to agree with Charlotte Brontë that 'The passions are perfectly unknown to her'? Certainly the surface of the novels does not immediately suggest strong passions. Jane Austen, in choosing to delineate as accurately as possible the life she knew, recognized that that life was not likely to include mad wives,

French mistresses, storms, orphanings and the rest of the paraphernalia of the romantic novel. Her prime belief that one should come to terms with the reality of life, that one should deal only with what was probable, is as much part of her first published novel, *Sense and Sensibility*, as it is of *Emma*. And since her settings are the drawing-rooms, ballrooms, parks and gardens of a civilized, leisured class, she was unlikely to introduce lunatics, villains or ghostly figures—they could only very occasionally have crossed her path!

But if we are content only with the superficial urbanity and humour we miss a great deal, for her insight constantly takes her beneath the surface of social life.

HER PERCEPTION

On the level of social behaviour, for example, we have to follow Jane Austen closely. A single word will indicate that she has observed the significant motivation that lies beneath an unobtrusive action. Thus she can write in *Pride and Prejudice*:

> Miss Lucas perceived him [Mr. Collins] from an upper window as he walked towards the house, and instantly set out to meet him *accidentally* in the lane. (my italics)   22, 121

In this way does an intelligent, quiet, young woman take her fate into her own hands—the best fate she can see for herself. And with the same economy, Jane Austen portrays the shrewdness of Mr. Shepherd in *Persuasion*:

> . . . a civil, cautious lawyer, who, whatever might be his hold or his views on Sir Walter, would rather have the *disagreeable* prompted by any body else. . . .   2, 11.

She has a quick ear for the minor embarrassments and misunderstandings of social intercourse:

> 'Ah! he has got a partner. I wish he had asked *you*', said Mrs] Allen. And after a short silence, she added, 'he [Henry Tilney is a very agreeable young man.'
> 'Indeed he is, Mrs. Allen', said Mrs. Thorpe, smiling complacently; 'I must say it, though I *am* his mother, that there is not a more agreeable young man in the world.'

This inapplicable answer might have been too much for the comprehension of many; but it did not puzzle Mrs. Allen, for after only a moment's consideration, she said, in a whisper to Catherine, 'I dare say she thought I was speaking of her son.'

NORTHANGER ABBEY 8, 58-59

And in *Persuasion*, the dramatic moment when Lady Russell is to see again—the first time for many years—the Captain Wentworth whom she had persuaded Anne to reject, becomes a moment of ironic mischance, truer to reality and to the characters involved than a dramatic rencounter. Anne, with Lady Russell in her carriage, sees him in the street:

> . . . it was not to be supposed that Lady Russell would perceive him till they were nearly opposite. She looked at her however, from time to time, anxiously; and when the moment approached which must point him out . . . she was yet perfectly conscious of Lady Russell's eyes being turned exactly in the direction for him, of her being in short intently observing him. . . .
> At last, Lady Russell drew back her head.—'Now, how would she speak of him?'
> 'You will wonder,' said she, 'what has been fixing my eye so long; but I was looking after some window-curtains, which Lady Alicia and Mrs. Frankland were telling me of last night.'

19, 179

Jane Austen is always aware of those nuances of feeling and half-unspoken clashes of personality that occur in any social gathering. Thus, when her brother-in-law visits Hartfield with his family, Emma is on tenterhooks in case her father's idiosyncrasies should irritate John Knightley and cause him to speak sharply, which would upset Mr. Woodhouse. Several times during the evening, she effectively changes the course of the conversation to avoid this, but eventually it has to happen:

> 'Ah! my dear, as Perry says, where health is at stake, nothing else should be considered; and if one is to travel, there is not much to chuse between forty miles and an hundred. . . .'
> 'Mr. Perry . . . would do as well to keep his opinion till it is asked for. . . . If Mr. Perry can tell me how to convey a wife and five children a distance of an hundred and thirty miles with no

41

greater expense or inconvenience than a distance of forty, I
should be as willing to prefer Cromer to South End as he could
himself.' ...

Mr. Woodhouse was rather agitated by such harsh reflections
on his friend Perry. ...   EMMA *12*, 106-107

For Jane Austen an emotion is rarely simple. When Harriet
brings her trophy of the court plaster to Emma to be burnt, we
are involved not only in Harriet's foolish affectation of romantic
love, but in Emma's remorse that she encouraged it, as well as
in the ironic comment contained in the memento itself—the
fact that it is only a bit of sticking plaster that the silly girl is
worshipping. And in *Persuasion*, the happy Christmas atmosphere at the Musgroves is anathema to Lady Russell:

> On one side was a table, occupied by some chattering girls,
> cutting up silk and gold paper; and on the other were tressels
> and trays, bending under the weight of brawn and cold pies,
> where riotous boys were holding high revel; the whole com-
> pleted by a roaring Christmas fire. ...
> 'I hope I shall remember, in future,' said Lady Russell, as
> soon as they were reseated in the carriage, 'not to call at Upper-
> cross in the Christmas holidays.'
> Every body has their taste in noises as well as in other matters.
> ... When Lady Russell, not long afterwards, was entering Bath
> on a wet afternoon, and driving through the long course of
> streets from the Old Bridge to Camden-place, amidst the dash
> of other carriages, the heavy rumble of carts and drays, the
> bawling of newsmen, muffin-men and milkmen, and the cease-
> less clink of pattens, she made no complaint.   *14*, 134-135

EMOTIONS WITHIN THE SOCIAL FRAMEWORK

Jane Austen knows that in society emotion can be expressed
through a look or an action without a word being said:

> She saw that he saw Elizabeth, that Elizabeth saw him, that there
> was complete internal recognition on each side; she was con-
> vinced that he was ready to be acknowledged as an acquaintance,
> expecting it, and she had the pain of seeing her sister turn away
> with unalterable coldness.   PERSUASION *19*, 176

42

And sometimes, when the lightness and wit have been dropped, we become aware of her knowledge of the springs of human behaviour:

> Miss Bates stood in the very worst predicament in the world for having much of the public favour; and she had no intellectual superiority to make atonement to herself, or *frighten those who might hate her, into an outward respect.* (my italics)   EMMA 3, 21

This is a harsh condemnation of society's treatment of a poor, unmarried, rather foolish spinster—and after all, Jane Austen was a poor, unmarried spinster herself.

She was aware of those hurts—less important and certainly unobtrusive, but no less felt—that can be given in social intercourse. Frank Churchill, on Box Hill, humorously proposes that everyone should contribute 'two things moderately clever—or three things very dull indeed' to enliven the party. And Miss Bates exclaims: '. . . then I need not be uneasy. "Three things very dull indeed." That will just do for me, you know. I shall be sure to say three dull things as soon as ever I open my mouth, shan't I?' Emma retorts woundingly, 'Ah! ma'am, but there may be a difficulty. Pardon me—but you will be limited as to the number—only three at once.' Miss Bates' slight blush shows her pain, and she says, 'Ah!—well—to be sure. Yes, I see what she means, (turning to Mr. Knightley,) and I will try to hold my tongue. I must make myself very disagreeable, or she would not have said such a thing to an old friend' (*E. 43*, 370-371). We may laugh at her portrait of Mrs. Bennet, but she is quite serious when she comments: 'She [Mrs. Bennet] was a woman of mean understanding, little information, and uncertain temper' (*P. & P. 1*, 5).

The same harshness and impatience appear in her perception in Mrs. Musgrove's 'large fat sighings' over her dead son:

> The real circumstance of this pathetic piece of family history were, that the Musgroves had had the ill fortune of a very troublesome, hopeless son; and the good fortune to lose him before he reached his twentieth year . . . he had been very little cared for at any time by his family, though quite as much as he

> deserved . . . and scarcely at all regretted when the intelligence
> of his death abroad had worked its way to Uppercross, two years
> before. PERSUASION *6*, 50-51

And there is her clear-sighted recognition of the limitations of
human communication which suggests to her that even the most
sincere relationship, such as that between Emma and Mr.
Knightley, cannot be perfect and complete: 'Seldom, very
seldom, does complete truth belong to any human disclosure;
seldom can it happen that something is not a little disguised, or
a little mistaken . . .' (*E. 49*, 431).

These are the perceptions and conclusions that take her
beyond the façade of good manners. They reveal the springs of
human behaviour. They add the serious tone to her work, but
they also, at another level, make her a comic writer.

THE PASSIONS

The passions *do* appear in her novels. Marianne's sufferings over
Willoughby's desertion in *Sense and Sensibility* are presented
feelingly enough, even though they are seen only from the
outside, through Elinor's eyes, and then are proved selfish and
unfeeling displays. Anne's defence of the long-lasting powers
of a woman's love, towards the end of *Persuasion*, is as feeling
as any reader could wish, and Emma's sufferings at various
points in her history are considerable.

But emotion in Jane Austen's world must be controlled and
concealed—that is, violent emotion. It is a test of character
that though one feels deeply, one does not distress other people
by a display of feeling. Thus, although the passions are experienced in her novels, they are not made a subject for display.
They are disciplined, brought under the control of reason.

Anne Elliot, after reading Captain Wentworth's letter,
experiences 'an over-powering happiness', but social circumstances required that she should control it to the best of her
ability: 'The absolute necessity of seeming like herself produced
then an immediate struggle' (*P. 23*, 238). And when she reached
home: 'An interval of meditation, serious and grateful, was the

best corrective of every thing dangerous in such high-wrought felicity; and she went to her room, and grew steadfast and fearless in the thankfulness of her enjoyment' (23, 245). Such periods of solitude and contemplation are the habitual reactions of her heroines to moments of stress. The alternative is exercise or occupation. Elizabeth, after reading Darcy's letter, wanders 'along the lane for two hours, giving way to every variety of thought' until 'fatigue, and a recollection of her long absence, made her at length return home' (P. & P. 36, 209); and when she recovers from the shock of hearing of Lydia's elopement: 'Had Elizabeth been at leisure to be idle, she would have remained certain that all employment was impossible to one so wretched as herself; but she had her share of business . . .' (46, 281). Elinor, on the death of her father, is deeply afflicted but 'still she could struggle, she could exert herself. She could consult with her brother, could receive her sister-in-law . . .' (S. & S. 1, 7).

Emotion experienced and controlled is, therefore, a part of her novels. She does not exclude the passions from her work, but she is most interested in emotions which are experienced within a social framework and which find their expression within the conventions of that framework.

The wilder emotions and actions cannot be given free play within her novels, but she *can* give, with the minimum of rhetorical flourish, brilliant examples of other emotions, equally strong and of perhaps equal significance. Envy, jealousy, cunning, hypocrisy, pride, snobbery, and vanity will always be part of life. There are skilful studies of these emotions in a social setting, as true to human nature as when they are portrayed on a larger scale. She was aware of how much and how little honesty was possible in a social situation, and how small the circle of people to whom one could respond with sympathy and liking: 'There are few people whom I really love, and still fewer of whom I think well' (P. & P. 24, 135). But she did love some, and did think well of some, and she was aware also of the relationships and events, the good company, rich conversation, and the humour that could be placed on the credit side of society.

4

The Novels–I: 'Northanger Abbey', 'Sense and Sensibility', 'Pride and Prejudice'

In this chapter and in the next, I shall give a brief consideration of each of Jane Austen's published novels. This is intended mainly to be a basis for the discussion of wider considerations which follows.

Northanger Abbey

It is convenient to begin with this novel, not because it was the first published (it did not appear until after her death), but because it derives most obviously from her reaction to the popular novel of her time, and in this is most closely related to her earliest writing. It was begun in 1797 or 1798, was then known as *Susan* and was sold in 1803 to Crosby the publisher. But it obviously underwent a great deal of revision after it was bought back from him and is, therefore, a book which was being written during most of her adult life.

It apparently began as a burlesque of the contemporary novel of horror and of sentiment, and much of the story still depends on this—there is a great deal of parody and burlesque still there. But the novel moves from this concern with literature to a concern with life, and so it follows Jane Austen's own development as a writer.

THEMES AND STRUCTURE—CATHERINE AS ANTI-HEROINE
These are the two themes which determine the novel's structure, and Catherine Morland, the heroine, is central to both. Catherine has first to learn to distinguish between literature and life, and

then has to learn the difficulties of ordinary life. The two themes are clearly announced. Chapter I begins: 'No one who had ever seen Catherine Morland in her infancy, would have supposed her born to be an heroine' (*1*, 13); and when Catherine is disabused of her romantic fancies, the second theme is announced: 'The anxieties of common life began soon to succeed to the alarms of romance' (*25*, 201).

Catherine is the anti-heroine in that, although she is to be the heroine of this novel, she has none of the characteristics of the conventional fictional heroine—no beauty, intellect, mysterious background—not even a lover. If we compare her with Emmeline, the heroine of the currently popular *Orphan of the Castle*, we find how conspicuously Catherine lacks the attainments necessary for a heroine.

Emmeline formed correct literary tastes in a ruined library and had 'of every useful ornamental feminine employment . . . long since made herself mistress without any instruction'. But Catherine Morland 'never could learn or understand any thing before she was taught; and sometimes not even then, for she was often inattentive, and occasionally stupid' (*1*, 14). Emmeline learnt to play the harp only by listening to someone else receiving instruction in that instrument, and with no more instruction in drawing could execute a perfect portrait of her lover, leaving it on the pianoforte for him to find. Catherine, on the other hand, only progressed so far in musical appreciation as to be able to 'listen to other people's performance with very little fatigue' (*1*, 16), and 'Her greatest deficiency was in the pencil—she had no notion of drawing—not enough even to attempt a sketch of her lover's profile, that she might be detected in the design'. And if we remember all the difficulties encountered by Evelina in Fanny Burney's novel when this young lady first visits London and Bath, we will understand why Mrs. Morland, when Catherine goes to Bath, has no idea of warning her against the violence of noblemen and baronets, but only begs her daughter to wrap herself up very warm about the throat when she comes from the Rooms at night, and to try to keep some account of the money she spends.

Yet in spite of her disadvantages, Catherine is destined to be a heroine—a heroine in terms of common life.

THE LAWS OF PROBABILITY

The first part of the novel is conceived of in terms of the opposition between fact and fiction. The structure here is, therefore, determined by the structure of the contemporary novel. Like Fanny Burney's Evelina, Catherine must be introduced into society—in this case, the sophistication of Bath. Like Evelina, her ignorance and innocence cause her some embarrassments and troubles. She meets the hero, Henry Tilney, who constantly makes fun of the conventions of the popular novel to her, and of the correct behaviour for a heroine:

> 'I see what you think of me,' said he gravely—'I shall make but a poor figure in your journal tomorrow. . . . Friday, went to the Lower Rooms; wore my sprigged muslin robe with blue trimmings—plain black shoes—appeared to much advantage; but was strangely harassed by a queer, half-witted man, who would make me dance with him, and distressed me by his nonsense.' *3, 26*

At Bath, she also finds the friend and confidante necessary to a sentimental heroine in Isabella Thorpe, who helps her extend her reading in Gothic fiction by providing her with a reading list of the most popular novels:

> The progress of the friendship between Catherine and Isabella was quick as its beginning had been warm, and they passed so rapidly through every gradation of increasing tenderness, that there was shortly no fresh proof of it to be given to their friends or themselves. They called each other by their Christian name, were always arm in arm when they walked, pinned up each other's train for the dance, and were not to be divided in the set. . . .
>
> *5, 36-37*

John Thorpe, Isabella's brother, and James Morland, Catherine's brother, who are friends at university (though Catherine had not known of this previously) arrive in Bath together. The behaviour of the Thorpes causes some embarrassment to Catherine where Henry Tilney and his sister are concerned, but Isabella's engagement to James gives her great happiness.

Unknown to Catherine, General Tilney, Henry's father, has been told by John Thorpe that Catherine is an heiress, and as a result Catherine is invited by the Tilneys to stay with them at their home, Northanger Abbey:

> Her passion for ancient edifices was next in degree to her passion for Henry Tilney—and castles and abbies made usually the charm of those reveries which his image did not fill. . . . With all the chances against her of house, hall, place, park, court, and cottage, Northanger turned up an abbey, and she was to be its inhabitant. Its long, damp passages, its narrow cells and ruined chapel, were to be within her daily reach, and she could not entirely subdue the hope of some traditional legends, some awful memorials of an injured and ill-fated nun. *17, 141*

Before she leaves Bath, Catherine is aware of a change in Isabella's attitude to James—some unkind behaviour, and a weakness for flirting with Captain Tilney—which disturbs her for her brother's sake.

Up to this point, Catherine has undergone many of the trials of the sentimental heroine, but always in a realistic and probable fashion. She has been prevented from dancing by John Thorpe, teased into riding with him when she ought to have been walking with the Tilneys, and generally led into small mistakes of courtesy. But none of them are serious, and many possible troubles she misses entirely because she is too simple and honest to see them.

During the drive to the Abbey, Henry continues his satire on the horror novel by telling her what she, as a heroine, might expect on her arrival: 'And are you prepared to encounter all the horrors that a building such as "what one reads about" may produce?—Have you a stout heart?—Nerves fit for sliding panels and tapestry?' (*20, 157-158*). He goes on to talk of a remote and gloomy chamber in which she is to sleep, of 'a ponderous chest', and of 'Dorothy the ancient housekeeper'.

After this, it is a set piece of irony on Jane Austen's part that the Abbey should be modern:

> An abbey!—yes, it was delightful to be really in an abbey!—but she doubted, as she looked round the room, whether any thing within her observation, would have given her the consciousness. The furniture was in all the profusion and elegance of modern taste. The fire-place . . . was contracted to a Rumford, with slabs of plain though handsome marble, and ornaments over it of the prettiest English china. . . .   20, 161-162

Yet it is not surprising that Catherine's imagination is allowed full play, and that she sees mysteries where none exist. General Tilney, suspected by her of murdering his wife or at least of having locked her up somewhere in the house, takes on 'the air and attitude of a Montoni', the sinister owner of the Castle of Udolpho in Mrs. Radcliffe's novel. The burlesque here is all intended to reveal to Catherine that she is imaginatively at fault. In each instance where her imagination has transformed an object or incident into an aspect of a horror novel, she is eventually shown that the object or incident is commonplace, or, if it has a significance which is unpleasant, it is unpleasant in terms of common life. Thus General Tilney may not be a wife-murderer, but he is a selfishly ambitious man.

It is Henry who eventually disabuses Catherine of her confusion of literature with life—'Remember the country and the age in which we live. Remember that we are English, that we are Christians. Consult your own understanding, your own sense of the probable . . .' (24, 197).

The burlesquing of literature ends with Volume II Chapter X (Chapter 25 in other editions), when Catherine is finally awakened to the dangers of confusing life with literature—'The visions of romance were over'. And in the same chapter the second theme is taken up more strongly and forms the basis of the rest of the book. This is the theme of education into real life—into human nature and human behaviour. It has been part of the earlier chapters also, but it comes out strongly again with James' letter telling Catherine that he has been jilted by Isabella.

The difficulties of real life increase when the General, who has now learnt that Catherine is not an heiress, expels her from his house and she is consequently separated from Henry.

THE EDUCATION OF CATHERINE

These two themes are linked in that they centre on Catherine and the educative process which is to mature her. She learns not to be deceived by literature, and not to be deceived by life. Catherine is inadequate as a fictional heroine, missing opportunity after opportunity to suffer, to act, to confide in the way of the sentimental heroines of the age. She refuses to be persuaded into love by Isabella:

> 'But you should not persuade me that I think so very much about Mr. Tilney, for perhaps I may never see him again.'
> 'Not see him again! My dearest creature, do not talk of it. I am sure you would be miserable if you thought so.'
> 'No, indeed, I should not.'   *6*, 41

She is blind to the idea of Isabella being in love with her brother, in spite of her friend's hints:

> 'Well, my taste is different. I prefer light eyes; and as to complexion—do you know—I like a sallow better than any other. You must not betray me, if you should ever meet with one of your acquaintance answering that description.'
> 'Betray you!—What do you mean?'
> 'Nay, do not distress me. I believe I have said too much. Let us drop the subject.'   *6*, 42

Isabella, who apes the sentimental heroine in her speech and manners, can impose on Catherine's simplicity for a time:

> 'Had I the command of millions, were I mistress of the whole world, your brother would be my only choice.'
> This charming sentiment, recommended as much by sense as novelty, gave Catherine a most pleasing remembrance of all the heroines of her acquaintance. . . .   *15*, 119

Catherine is gullible because of her nature. She is 'Open, candid, artless, guileless, with affections strong but simple, forming no pretensions, and knowing no disguise' (25, 206). But her natural simplicity and directness is not always taken in by Isabella, John Thorpe, or General Tilney, and her insight into character is not always mistaken.

However, it is necessary for her to be more perceptive, to be educated so that she can no longer be imposed upon by literature or life. She is educated into a love of beauty by Miss Tilney, and into understanding of character by Henry. She learns not to take at its face value what people say and do, but to look beneath at character and motive. Thus, Isabella's final letter to her can no longer deceive:

'I see what she has been about. She is a vain coquette, and her tricks have not answered. I do not believe she had ever any regard either for James or for me, and I wish I had never known her. . . . There is but one thing that I cannot understand. I see that she has had designs on Captain Tilney, which have not succeeded; but I do not understand what Captain Tilney has been about all this time. Why should he pay her such attentions as to make her quarrel with my brother, and then fly off himself?'

'I have very little to say for Frederick's motives, such as I believe them to have been. He has his vanities as well as Miss Thorpe, and the chief difference is, that, having a stronger head, they have not yet injured himself. If the *effect* of his behaviour does not justify him with you, we had better not seek after the cause.'

'Then you do not suppose he ever really cared about her?'

'I am persuaded that he never did.'

'And only made believe to do so for mischief's sake?'

Henry bowed his assent.

'Well, then, I must say that I do not like him at all.'

27, 218-219

Catherine is Jane Austen's most innocent heroine. She has none of the certainty of Elizabeth Bennet, none of the gentler perception of Anne Elliot, none of the righteousness of Fanny Price. She is closer in nature to Harriet Smith. But she is like Emma Woodhouse in that her ignorance catches her up in mistakes and misjudgements, so that the reader is always ahead of her in perception. From this derives, as in *Emma*, much of the irony of plot.

OTHER CHARACTERS

It is usual in a Jane Austen novel to find one character who in his perception, judgement and common-sense represents what is right. Henry Tilney is that character in this novel. He is able to see Catherine's errors and misjudgements and correct them. It is to him that she can turn for advice.

The other characters are seen in terms of the conventional characters of the popular novel, but at the same time they are realistic—probable. Mrs. Allen is at once the chaperon who *can*not or *will* not protect her young companion from social mishap and danger, and the lazy, indolent, dress-conscious woman of real life. As such she is an anti-chaperon.

Catherine has two women friends—Isabella Thorpe who figures at the beginning, and Miss Tilney who predominates in the second part. Isabella Thorpe is the conventional friend of the heroine of the popular novel who supports her, confides in her, and helps her. And this is the mask Isabella wears. But underneath is the shrewd, calculating, vulgar young woman looking out for a husband with money and not too particular about how she gets him. Isabella is the anti-confidante and the real-life social climber. Her friendship for Catherine, though insisted upon by her, is never convincing.

Miss Tilney, on the other hand, has all the virtues of taste, manners, judgement, correct behaviour and feeling. Her friendship for Catherine, though not fussed about, is a more genuine and lasting affair. Yet Miss Tilney is just a little too good to be true, and ironically, in this way, approximates most closely to the fictional heroine. Jane Austen is suggesting this when, at the end of the novel, she writes:

> The marriage of Eleanor Tilney, her removal from all the evils of such a home as Northanger had been made by Henry's banishment, to the home of her choice and the man of her choice, is an event which I expect to give general satisfaction among all her acquaintance. My own joy on the occasion is very sincere.

I know no one more entitled, by unpretending merit, or better prepared by habitual suffering, to receive and enjoy felicity.

31, 250-251

John Thorpe is the wag, the beau of the sentimental novels who embarrasses the heroine by his unwanted attentions and rudenesses, but he is a real enough young man, stupid, boorish and unpleasant. He is much stupider than his sister, but also has his pretensions—he puts on the airs of the fashionable young man about town, and his extravagant statements about his horses are one of the things that Catherine finds irreconcilable with truth.

General Tilney, though he *has* overtones of the Montoni-type villain, is primarily an embodiment of the vanity and mercenari-ness that Jane Austen disliked, and even Catherine's simplicity cannot be imposed upon by him for long. In many ways his is the voice of Sir Walter Elliot. Her compliments on his break-fast set bring the response that he 'confessed it to be neat and simple. . . . But this was quite an old set, purchased two years ago. . . . and had he not been perfectly without vanity of that kind, [he] might have been tempted to order a new set' (*22*, 175). As to his gardens, though he is 'without any ambitions of that sort himself—without any solicitude about it—he did believe them to be unrivalled in the kingdom' (*22*, 178). And he is like Dr. Grant in that, although he declares himself 'careless enough in most matters of eating', when he dines at Henry's house at Woodston, 'She could not but observe that the abundance of the dinner did not seem to create the smallest astonishment in the General; nay, that he was even looking at the side-table for cold meat which was not there. His son and daughter . . . had seldom seen him eat so heartily at any table but his own; and never before known him so little disconcerted by the melted butter's being oiled' (*26*, 214-215).

The minor characters in this novel are, therefore, all related to the double theme of the novel—the conflict between reality and literature, and the opposing conception of real-life disturb-ances being just as disturbing as fictional ones. And on this second level they portray all the customary targets of Jane's irony—stupidity and indolence, deceit, vulgarity, shrewdness, vanity and mercenariness.

TYPICAL METHODS

Two techniques which are typical of Jane Austen appear in this novel. The first is the use of the letter to communicate a *dénouement*. Catherine is withdrawn from the scene of the sub-plot when she leaves Bath for Northanger Abbey, and she must therefore receive the news of her brother's broken engagement and Isabella's attempt to re-instate herself with the Morlands, by letter. Elizabeth Bennet, in *Pride and Prejudice*, is similarly situated—she learns of Lydia's elopement by letter, and later of how Wickham was persuaded to marry her, by the same means. Fanny Price is also away from the main action, and receives intelligence by a newspaper report and by letter.

The second technique is Jane Austen's ironic withdrawal from her characters once the story reaches its conclusion. She clears up outstanding issues by an ironic and swift disclosure of the future, which distances everything and puts the characters firmly within the covers of a book:

> The anxiety, which in this state of their attachment must be the portion of Henry and Catherine, and of all who loved either, as to its final event, can hardly extend, I fear, to the bosom of my readers, who will see in the tell-tale compression of the pages before them, that we are all hastening together to perfect felicity. *31, 250*

This seems to reflect her impatience with the conventions of the novel which demand always such 'felicity' at the end. For her the interest of the novel seems to lie in the delineation and play of character according to what she conceives of as probable. She will bring this out even to the detriment of her heroine:

> ... though Henry was now sincerely attached to her. .... I must confess that his affection originated in nothing better than gratitude. ... It is a new circumstance in romance, I acknowledge, and dreadfully derogatory of an heroine's dignity; but if it be

as new in common life, the credit of a wild imagination will at
least be all my own.   *30, 243*

In *Northanger Abbey* Jane Austen satirises the more exaggerated conventions and excesses of the Gothic and sentimental
novel, but although she here makes her stand on realism, she
could not throw off entirely the conventions of romance. Hero
and heroine must come together in happiness, and while she
adapted the framework to her own ends, her impatience with it
does at times show through.

Sense and Sensibility

Like *Northanger Abbey*, this novel was written over a period of
many years, and probably has its origins in Jane Austen's
earliest writings. Its main theme—the dangers of sensibility
in temperament—suggests that it derives from an early concern
with the increasing popularity of this attitude in romantic
literature and an attempt on Jane Austen's part to discredit it
by pointing out its dangers and the advantages of 'sense'.

THEME AND STRUCTURE

This double theme of sense and sensibility has the disadvantage
of conjuring up double heroines and a double plot. Marianne
and Elinor Dashwood must each be shown pursuing her private
fate according to her individual outlook and belief. The fate in
each case is an unhappy love story, but this provides us with
parallel plots, demonstrations of the dual thesis, which is one
of the faults of the novel.

The story takes some time to get off the ground—it is
Chapter 6 before the Dashwoods are settled at Barton—but
character and theme are firmly presented in the opening chapters.
'Marianne's abilities were, in many respects, quite equal to
Elinor's. She was sensible and clever; but eager in every thing:
her sorrows, her joys, could have no moderation. She was
generous, amiable, interesting: she was every thing but prudent'
(*1, 6*). Elinor, on the other hand 'possessed a strength of understanding, and coolness of judgement. . . . She had an excellent

heart;—her disposition was affectionate, and her feelings were strong; but she knew how to govern them' (1, 6). At the death of her father she does this, while her mother and sister give themselves up to an 'excess of sensibility'.

Forced to leave their home, Norland Park, which has been inherited by their step-brother, the Dashwoods accept Sir John Middleton's offer of a house. Marianne and Elinor have no fortune, again as a result of their step-brother's meanness, and this is to be the stumbling block in their romantic adventures.

The theme of sense begins with the relationship between Edward Ferrars and Elinor which Marianne finds so odd because neither shows much emotion:

> 'Esteem him! Like him! Cold-hearted Elinor! Oh! worse than cold-hearted! Ashamed of being otherwise. Use those words again and I will leave the room this moment.'
> Elinor could not help laughing. . . . 'I am by no means assured of his regard for me. . . . In my heart I feel little—scarcely any doubt of his preference. But there are other points to be considered besides his inclination. He is very far from being independent . . . and I am very much mistaken if Edward is not himself aware that there would be many difficulties in his way, if he were to wish to marry a woman who had not either a great fortune or high rank.' 4, 21-22

Elinor's caution and Edward's reserve are opposed to Marianne's impetuosity and Willoughby's out-spokenness. Willoughby enters the novel in the guise of the true romantic hero— 'Marianne's preserver'—having carried her home when she sprained her ankle, and having all the energy, enthusiasm, taste, and sensibility that Marianne could desire.

The two plots are now carefully interwoven. Marianne's romance appears to flourish with all possible unconventionality until Willoughby leaves, and she is in anguish. Elinor's romance does not progress. She learns that Edward is secretly engaged to Lucy Steele, and she is forced to listen to Lucy Steele's confidences. The move to London, which brings about the final break with Willoughby, the revelation of his true character, and Marianne's severe sorrow, is followed by the insults Elinor receives from Edward's mother, and by the success of Lucy with that lady. The final outcome follows Marianne's illness and near death, and Lucy's elopement with Edward's brother.

We are involved, therefore, in alternate testing of each sister on the grounds of her love: Marianne's reaction is always the wild, irrational one, Elinor's the controlled, sensible one. While Marianne is so debilitated by grief that she easily catches a putrid fever, Elinor is able to pass on to Edward Colonel Brandon's kindness in presenting him with a small living, and she can go so far as to leave Lucy and Edward alone together.

Sense is justified, sensibility shown as weakness. And there is an ironic twist to these two plots. Romantic Marianne suffers, no doubt, but she comes eventually to a prosaic marriage with Colonel Brandon, while Elinor, the sensible Cinderella, is involved in all the trappings of the romantic plot—losing her lover, forced to listen to confidences from Lucy, despised by his mother, and eventually united to him but living much more modestly than Marianne and Colonel Brandon.

THE CONFLICT

We are intended to sympathise with Elinor and her standards and to see the weakness of Marianne's situation. The plot itself bears this out. And yet we do not. There is something very attractive about Marianne, and something too cold and smug about Elinor. This was obviously not what Jane Austen intended, but the problem is the same as that in *Mansfield Park*—the difficulty of making a 'good' character likeable when the best lines have to go to the flawed character. Marianne, with her outspokenness and spontaneity, is pleasanter to us, and those things she accuses Elinor of are not untrue:

> 'But I see what you mean. I have been too much at my ease, too happy, too frank. I have erred against every common-place notion of decorum . . . had I talked only of the weather and the roads, and had I spoken only once in ten minutes, this reproach would have been spared.'   5, 48

> 'But I thought it was right . . . to be guided wholly by the opinion of other people. I thought our judgements were given us merely

to be subservient to those of our neighbours. This has always
been your doctrine I am sure.'   *17*, 93-94

And certainly there is something like hypocrisy in Elinor's
calmness, in her manoeuvring to question Lucy Steele further
about Edward (if Lucy is playing a game in confessing, Elinor
is playing a similar game in concealing her feelings), and in
leaving Lucy and Edward together, even loitering on the stairs
to give them more time alone.

It is true that Jane Austen tries to counteract this effect. In
general, the two sisters agree about their acquaintances—Mrs.
Jennings' vulgarity, for example. Marianne responds by ignoring
them, by being brusque and rude, while Elinor always remains
good-mannered.

> Lady Middleton proposed a rubber of Casino to the others·
> No one made any objection but Marianne, who, with her usual
> inattention to the forms of general civility, exclaimed, 'Your
> ladyship will have the goodness to excuse *me*—you know I
> detest cards. I shall go to the piano-forté; I have not touched it
> since it was tuned.' And without further ceremony, she turned
> away and walked to the instrument.
>
> Lady Middleton looked as if she thanked heaven that *she* had
> never made so rude a speech.
>
> 'Marianne can never keep long from that instrument you
> know, ma'am', said Elinor, endeavouring to smooth away the
> offence; 'and I do not much wonder at it; for it is the very best
> toned piano-forté I ever heard.'
>
> 23, 144-145

(But this sounds suspiciously like Lucy Steele.) And when the
two sisters go to London with Mrs. Jennings:

> ... Marianne's behaviour as they travelled was a happy specimen
> of what her future complaisance and companionableness to
> Mrs. Jennings might be expected to be. She sat in silence almost
> all the way, wrapt in her own meditations, and scarcely ever
> voluntarily speaking. ... To atone for this conduct therefore,
> Elinor took immediate possession of the post of civility which
> she had assigned herself, behaved with the greatest attention to

Mrs. Jennings, talked with her, laughed with her, and listened to her whenever she could. . . .

26, 160

But Elinor is also given a strain of ironic humour:

> '. . . and for my part', [says Lucy Steele] 'I love to see children full of life and spirits; I cannot bear them if they are tame and quiet.'
>
> 'I confess', replied Elinor, 'that while I am at Barton Park, I never think of tame and quiet children with any abhorrence.'

21, 122-123

When Marianne rhapsodises about the fallen leaves at Norland, Elinor retorts: 'It is not everyone who has your passion for dead leaves'. When Mrs. Jennings comes with the glass of old Constantia wine to comfort Marianne and her broken heart only to find she is sleeping, Elinor offers to drink the wine, and she 'reflected that, though its good effects on a cholicky gout were, at present, of little importance to her, its healing powers on a disappointed heart might be as reasonably tried on herself as on her sister' (30, 198). If this strain had been further developed we might have sympathised rather more with Elinor. Jane Austen is happiest when her heroine is the flawed but vivacious character, like Elizabeth and Emma, and the good character is in a secondary position like Jane Bennet.

OTHER CHARACTERS

Edward Ferrars and Willoughby parallel Elinor and Marianne. Edward is sensible, though, as a very young man with little to occupy him, he was so 'unsensible' as to engage himself to Lucy. Willoughby, to all intents and purposes, is at first the 'sentimental' hero—dashing, passionate, enthusiastic. Both young men are similarly situated in that their futures are under the direction of a female relative who has control of their fortunes. Edward, in spite of being disowned by his mother, honours his promises to Lucy and is willing to marry her without love—or money. Willoughby (whose sensibility is only a pretence), having been disinherited also, rejects Marianne and marries a woman of fortune. The same irony exists as in the case of Elinor and Marianne—the sensible hero makes the romantic gesture, the sentimental hero makes the worldly gesture.

Perhaps because so much of the novel is taken up by Marianne's intense grief and illness, *Sense and Sensibility* has a more sombre air than *Northanger Abbey*. It has its comic characters, but one or two of them are unpleasant. The Misses Steele are noted for their vulgarity. In addition, the younger is shrewd and the elder is stupid. They are both stigmatised by grammatical lapses in speaking and writing as well as by lapses into bad taste generally. Miss Steele is particularly prone to these faults. There is something grating about Miss Steele, as there is about Lucy, and there can be something very *unfunny* about the Barton party generally—perhaps because the Misses Dashwood find the company at the Park so trying. Certainly, the conversation at the Park is not brilliant:

> When they were seated in the dining room, Sir John observed with regret that they were only eight altogether.
>
> 'My dear', said he to his lady, 'it is very provoking that we should be so few. Why did not you ask the Gilberts to come to us today?'
>
> 'Did not I tell you, Sir John, when you spoke to me about it before, that it could not be done? They dined with us last.'
>
> 'You and I, Sir John', said Mrs. Jennings, 'should not stand upon such ceremony.'
>
> 'Then you would be very ill-bred', cried Mr. Palmer.
>
> 'My love, you contradict every body',—said his wife with her usual laugh. 'Do you know that you are quite rude?'
>
> 'I did not know I contradicted any body in calling your mother ill-bred.'
>
> 'Aye, you may abuse me as you please', said the good-natured old lady, 'you have taken Charlotte off my hands, and cannot give her back again. So there I have the whip hand of you.'
>
> Charlotte laughed heartily to think that her husband could not get rid of her. . . .

20, III-II2

Mrs. Dashwood's sensibility and concern for her daughters' happiness is contrasted with Mrs. Jennings' common-sense. Whereas Mrs. Dashwood rejects the idea of deliberately making matches and ensnaring young men, Mrs. Jennings is always match-making, and has the satisfaction of having married off two not very promising daughters successfully. Mrs. Ferrars, as a mother, is selfish, designing and cold-hearted, but approaches burlesque in her habit of disinheriting her sons. This seems to link her with the wicked parents and guardians of the contemporary novel:

> Her family had of late been exceedingly fluctuating. For many years of her life she had had two sons; but the crime and annihilation of Edward a few weeks ago, had robbed her of one; the similar annihilation of Robert had left her for a fortnight without any; and now, by the resuscitation of Edward, she had one again. *50, 373*

THE CONVENTIONS

There are aspects of this novel which seem to depend upon the conventional novel—some of them are tedious here, some are treated with impatient irony by Jane Austen.

There is, for example, the young woman ruined by her association with a ruthless young man. In this case it is Colonel Brandon's ward. These seductions frequently happen at seaside resorts, or at Bath. Miss Williams, at Bath, was 'ranging over the town and making what acquaintance [she] chose' (*31, 209*). Lydia (in *Pride and Prejudice*) is on a visit to Brighton when she meets Wickham again, and Miss Darcy was at Ramsgate when he attempted to elope with her.

A further convention is the inset story that is pathetic and necessary for a full understanding of the plot or of motive. Jane Austen satirized this convention when she wrote in *Northanger Abbey* of Mrs. Thorpe:

> This brief account of the family is intended to supersede the necessity of a long and minute detail from Mrs. Thorpe herself of her past adventures and sufferings, which might otherwise be expected to occupy the three or four following chapters; in

which the worthlessness of lords and attornies might be set
forth, and conversations, which had passed twenty years before,
be minutely repeated.   4, 34

No doubt the inset stories in *Sense and Sensibility* are of greater
necessity to the plot than Mrs. Thorpe's history is to *Northanger
Abbey*, but they are a clumsy means of filling up the gaps. In
this instance we have Colonel Brandon's story, Edward Ferrars'
story, and eventually Willoughby's story. In *Persuasion*, Mrs.
Smith's story of Mr. Elliot is an even greater imposition on the
novel. In *Pride and Prejudice* we require Darcy's letter, and also
Wickham's story. In *Emma*, a more neatly constructed novel,
there is only Frank Churchill's letter.

I think we can conclude that this novel is not one of her
successes. The didactic theme splits plot and characterisation,
leaving us with no entirely sympathetic heroine. The tone is
more sombre, even the comic characters more grating than
comic. And the emphasis upon the banality of social visits
suggests that Jane Austen was then finding social intercourse
boring, though, like Elinor, she probably tried to see the best
side of it.

Pride and Prejudice

Jane Austen took the title, and therefore the theme, of this novel
from Fanny Burney, who wrote of her novel *Cecilia*, 'The whole
unfortunate business' was 'the result of Pride and Prejudice'.
Mr. Darcy's excessive pride, his first proposal to Elizabeth, and
Lady Catherine's interview with her at Longbourn, were all
based on incidents in *Cecilia*.

THEMES AND STRUCTURE

Marriage is set as a theme of the novel in Chapter I, seen first
from the point of view of the mother out to find good matches
for her daughters. This is the first statement of the theme, and it
is developed through the plot, and through the various discussions of marriage which punctuate the story. But on the basis of
Mrs. Bennet's ambition are built two marriages of love which the

elder Bennet girls manage for themselves, one marriage of passion which Lydia manages for herself, and one marriage of convenience which Charlotte Lucas manages for herself. The irony lies, therefore, in Mrs. Bennet's complete inability to find her daughters husbands—indeed her vulgarity generally has the opposite effect and almost drives away suitors entirely.

But involved in this theme is the pride and prejudice motif, the feelings which come in the way of marriage as much as do Mrs. Bennet and her vulgarity.

As in *Sense and Sensibility* and *Northanger Abbey*, therefore, we have a didactic theme, a theme related to two dominant character traits, though not, in this case, necessarily related to contemporary fashions in literature. Moreover, the two character traits of pride and prejudice are now divided *not*, as in *Sense and Sensibility*, between two sisters, which is a static theme and can only function by parallel stories, but between a man and a woman, initially hostile to each other, eventually attracted to each other, which is a dynamic theme and functions by means of conflicts, confrontations and misunderstandings between the two. From the beginning of the novel we see the advantages of this change.

The viewpoint is the viewpoint of comedy. There may be dangers and difficulties to be overcome, but in a comic, witty world they will be overcome with the minimum of sorrow.

In Chapter 3 the theme of pride is introduced with the character of Darcy, his refusal to dance, his slighting of Elizabeth Bennet. And pride is discussed in Chapter 5 when Elizabeth points to the real unpleasantness of it.

> 'His pride,' said Miss Lucas, 'does not offend *me* so much as pride often does, because there is an excuse for it. One cannot wonder that so very fine a young man, with family, fortune, every thing in his favour, should think highly of himself. If I may so express it, he has a *right* to be proud.'
>
> 'That is very true', replied Elizabeth, 'and I could easily forgive *his* pride, if he had not mortified *mine*.' 5, 20

The antagonism which she feels for Darcy is expressed by verbal encounters between the two which demonstrate Elizabeth's wit. Only the reader is aware of his growing attraction for her—Elizabeth is blinded by her own antagonism. This reaches its climax with Wickham's story, which she accepts without question, and which leads to her rejection of Darcy's proposal. Darcy's first proposal, in fact, is the climax of pride on his part and prejudice on hers. From that point each works towards a fuller understanding of the other, so that the remainder of the novel is something of an anti-climax where their relationship is concerned. It requires all kinds of external action—the visit to Pemberley, Lydia's elopement, Darcy's rescuing of her, Lady Catherine's interference—to bring them together again. In none of these, except in the last instance, is there room for confrontations between them, or for Elizabeth's wit to shine. The action has moved away, and at the same time their personal relationship has gone underground into their minds and thoughts.

The parallel plot of Jane's romance, similar to Elinor's, goes on without disturbing the main course of the novel—it is on a subsidiary level. Jane never suffers the distress of Marianne because she is like Elinor, but we can accept this since Elizabeth holds the centre of the stage. In fact, we know that the Jane/Bingley affair depends upon the change of heart in the Elizabeth/Darcy affair.

The novel is brought to a close with the customary elopement, the horror it arouses, and, since this is a comedy, the marriage that results. And again we have the profusion of letters reporting these events, and Jane Austen's withdrawal from her characters at the end.

One interesting point of structure is the shortness of chapters, especially at the beginning of the novel, which makes for speed of movement, and the closeness to stage dialogue which is apparent in the beginning, which also makes for speed.

CANDOUR

We do not actually hear Elizabeth speak until Chapter 4, when she reveals herself at once as a lively young woman with an independent mind:

'Oh! you are a great deal too apt you know, to like people in general. You never see a fault in anybody. All the world are good and agreeable in your eyes. I never heard you speak ill of a human being in my life.'

'I would wish not to be hasty in censuring any one; but I always speak what I think.'

'I know you do; and it is *that* which makes the wonder. With *your* good sense, to be so honestly blind to the follies and non-sense of others! Affectation of candour is common enough;—one meets it every where. But to be candid without ostentation or design—to take the good of every body's character and make it still better, and say nothing of the bad—belongs to you alone.'

4, 14–15

The sisters are comparing their individual assessments of the characters of other people, with the Netherfield party particularly in mind. Elizabeth accuses her sister of 'candour', and of being 'candid without ostentation or design'.

The words 'candour' and 'candid' appear several times in Jane Austen's novels, and their meaning is of interest since it is connected with the grounds on which we judge the character of others—a question which involves her heroines particularly. The words, as she uses them, generally do not have simply the modern meaning of 'frankness, ingenuousness, sincerity in what one says', but have the added suggestion of an earlier meaning which involves kindliness, being favourably disposed to others, desiring to make the best of people and to put the best interpretations upon their words and actions: in Elizabeth's phrase, 'to take the good of every body's character and make it still better, and say nothing of the bad'.

The words bear the same meaning and assume the same importance in other novels. In *Sense and Sensibility*, Elinor Dashwood, discussing Colonel Brandon with Marianne and Willoughby, who 'seemed resolved to undervalue his merits', suggests to Willoughby that Colonel Brandon's 'observations have stretched much farther than *your* candour': i.e., than Willoughby's willingness to be kindly and generous in summing up his character.

In *Emma*, Frank Churchill is judged by the neighbourhood with great candour; liberal allowances were made for the little excesses of such a handsome young man—one who smiled so often and bowed so well'. But Mr. Knightley was 'not to be softened' from his powers of censure by 'bows or smiles'. And again, after Emma has insulted Miss Bates on Box Hill, the poor spinster nevertheless speaks of the incident 'with candour and generosity'. She honours Emma's forbearance in paying her attentions when her society must have been so irksome. Miss Bates, of course, is 'candid' where everybody is concerned.

Jane Austen is no more totally in favour of this kind of ingenuous judgement of human nature than she is of the lack of candour displayed on occasions by Marianne Dashwood, Emma, or Elizabeth Bennet. Both attitudes can lead to misapprehensions and misjudgements, and both need revision. Catherine Morland, in *Northanger Abbey*, must be educated into a less 'candid' view of human nature—one which can take account of the imperfections of mankind. But Elizabeth Bennet must learn to be more 'candid', less willing to think ill of people—especially of Darcy, because of the prejudice aroused by the initial insult he gives to her pride.

Elizabeth, coming from a background which has no moral standards—her mother is stupid and her father has ironically withdrawn from his natural responsibility for his family's moral welfare—has to rely on her own taste and commonsense and decision, and she is too sure of herself. Generally, her opinions of people are proved right. Only in three instances is she proved wrong—in the case of Charlotte Lucas, of Wickham, and of Darcy—but these are important cases. Her process of education in the novel is from prejudice to understanding, from lack of candour to a limited acceptance of its need.

THE DELUDED HEROINE

One of the advantages, structurally, that are obtained from having a heroine who is deluded is that there is an increase in irony, and the work takes on something of the interest of the detective story—the reader is given the same clues as the heroine as to

what is going on, and he can test his perception against hers
Thus we are given clues not only to Darcy's increasing love for
Elizabeth, but also to Charlotte's intentions towards Mr. Collins:

> [Elizabeth] owed her greatest relief to her friend Miss Lucas,
> who often joined them, and good-naturedly engaged Mr.
> Collins's conversation to herself. 18, 102

> . . . and again during the chief of the day, was Miss Lucas so
> kind as to listen to Mr. Collins. Elizabeth took an opportunity
> of thanking her. 'It keeps him in good humour', said she, 'and
> I am more obliged to you than I can express.' 22, 121

It is only at this point that we learn what Charlotte Lucas has
in mind. Similarly, the reader may, if he reads carefully enough,
see Wickham cautiously trying out the ground before he begins
to destroy Darcy's character. In doing so he 'affects candour' and
yet Elizabeth is not aware of his deception:

> 'Are you much acquainted with Mr. Darcy?'
> 'As much as I ever wish to be', cried Elizabeth warmly,—'I
> have spent four days in the same house with him, and I think
> him very disagreeable.'
> 'I have no right to give *my* opinion', said Wickham, 'as to
> his being agreeable or otherwise. I am not qualified to form one.
> I have known him too long and too well to be a fair judge. It is
> impossible for *me* to be impartial. But I believe your opinion
> of him would in general astonish- -and perhaps you would not
> express it quite so strongly any where else.—Here you are in
> your own family.'
> 'Upon my word I say no more *here* than I might say in any
> house in the neighbourhood, except Netherfield. . . .'
> 'I cannot pretend to be sorry', said Wickham, after a short
> interruption, 'that he or that any man should not be estimated
> beyond their deserts; but with *him* I believe it does not often
> happen. . . .' 16, 77-78

OTHER CHARACTERS

As in *Northanger Abbey* so in this novel, which probably gives
us the widest gallery of wholly comic minor characters of all,
the subsidiary characters tend to demonstrate further aspects of

the main themes. Thus we have the theme of pride and its adjunct, flattery and sycophancy, repeated in the characterisation. Darcy's status and his pride attract Miss Bingley who constantly flatters him and tries to ingratiate herself with him. There is no possibility of her succeeding in her aim of marrying him—he does not even seem to like her very much—and she lacks the shrewdness of a Lucy Steele in such matters. She is frequently discomfited, and does not cause Elizabeth any real unhappiness.

Lady Catherine de Bourgh is an extension of the Darcy pride to the limits of caricature. She has all his pride of family and position plus an unfailing sense of her own personal superiority:

> 'You know I always speak my mind, and I cannot bear the idea of two young women travelling post by themselves. . . . I have the greatest dislike in the world to that sort of thing. . . .'
>
> *37*, 211

It is a sad reflection on Lady Catherine's self-esteem that she requires and can tolerate a flatterer so obvious as Mr. Collins, who is the apotheosis of the sycophant, an out-and-out flatterer.

Mr. Collins' proposal to Elizabeth is in its way an early parody of Darcy's proposal. Mr. Collins, running through his reasons for marrying, can find three good ones without ever mentioning Elizabeth. And Mr. Darcy's proposal rests primarily on his sense of her inferiority, of the obstacles provided by her situation in life and by her family.

Mrs. Bennet is pure stupidity, and she develops a prejudice against Darcy stronger and more blind than Elizabeth's. Mary is perhaps the only comic character who is not a success—she makes only for tedium, but Mr. Bennet's wit is a strong civilising vein throughout.

Elizabeth is certainly attractive and convincing as a woman, and Jane in her own way is equally convincing, but the comic characters generally go too far towards caricature. And for this reason we often have the sense of the heroine moving among a world of grotesques—for example, Mr. Collins, Lady Catherine, Mrs. Bennet—who do not, on reflection, convince us of their truth to life.

5

The Novels–II: 'Mansfield Park', 'Emma', 'Persuasion'

Mansfield Park

Mansfield Park, published in 1814, a year after *Pride and Prejudice*, was probably being written while the latter novel was being revised, yet it provides a complete contrast in every way with the earlier novel. It is the most serious, and therefore the most controversial, of Jane Austen's novels and has come in for a good deal of criticism, though it also has its apologists.

In January 1813, Jane wrote to her sister: 'Now I will try to write of something else, & it shall be a complete change of subject—ordination . . .'. So we gather that the new seriousness of tone is deliberate and intended.

Ordination, admission to the ministry of the Church, *is* a serious subject, and it, together with the discussions of the profession of clergyman, enhances the seriousness of the novel. Mary Crawford and Edmund Bertram argue over Edmund's ordination. She is reluctant to come to terms with the idea of him as a clergyman, but it is what Fanny Price, the heroine, most approves of. Considering the clergymen who appear elsewhere in her novels, the seriousness here is unusual. Mr. Collins, Henry Tilney, Mr. Elton, Dr. Grant—none of these could, for varying reasons, be considered as models for the clergy. But it is not only ordination, but the whole question of Christian attitudes to life, which she takes up in this novel. Whereas in earlier novels mistakes of judgement might be made through defects of imagination or sensibility or prejudice or inability to see through the surface of manners, in this novel it requires an extremely narrow, undeviating sense of what is morally correct in order to pierce through the superficiality of appearance. Evil appears here in its most pleasant and attractive form in the characters of Mary and Henry Crawford—little wonder that the question of right judgement is such a difficult one, and the tone of the novel so serious.

THEMES AND STRUCTURE

The theme of the novel can be seen therefore as an examination of the validity of Christian attitudes to life. From this stem the many discussions of Christian concern that appear in the novel—the duties of the clergy, the importance of family prayers, etc. Benevolence, charity, good deeds are the beginning of the novel, centring round the adoption of nine-year-old Fanny Price. The conditions of the two sisters, Lady Bertram and Mrs. Price, are early established, one rich and the other poor, and out of the desire to help Mrs. Price comes the suggestion of the third sister, Mrs. Norris, that one of the Price children should be adopted: 'The trouble and expense of it to them, would be nothing compared with the benevolence of the action' (*1*, *5*). Sir Thomas Bertram hesitates on the grounds that the adopted child might contaminate his own family, but he is urged not to be frightened 'from a good deed by a trifle' (*1*, *6*). And, Fanny Price having been sent for, 'the pleasures of so benevolent a scheme were already enjoyed' (*1*, *8*).

Fanny is introduced into Mansfield Park, terrified and homesick, and completely misunderstood by its inhabitants. Their charity does not extend to an understanding of her predicament; she is simply a curiosity because of her silence or her ignorance, a means for the young Misses Bertram to show off their superior attainments, and an object for Mrs. Norris' scolding on her need to be grateful. Only her cousin Edmund perceives and understands her unhappiness, and helps her to get over it by showing how she can write a letter to her brother in Portsmouth. Fanny is retiring by nature, but she is also naturally good; she learns much from Edmund, who forms her taste, and above all she learns from her position the Christian virtues of humility and self-denial.

Suited to this Christian background, the structure of the book centres on a series of temptations, designed to test the virtue of the various characters. Mary and Henry Crawford—sociable, sophisticated, fascinating, and without moral principles—are staying with the Grants near Mansfield, and become the tempters. Edmund is so attracted by Mary as to overlook her faults and fall in love with her; Maria Bertram almost breaks her engagement to Mr. Rushworth because of Henry's attentions. The height of these temptations appears in the play they rehearse—encouraged by foolishness and vanity to act out in rehearsal their feelings in real life. Fanny refuses to take part.

The return of Sir Thomas Bertram from the West Indies ends these dangerous relationships, and when, later in the story, the Crawfords once more exert their influence at Mansfield, Maria is married and her sister Julia is with her in London. It is Fanny who is now subject to the temptation of Henry Crawford's love. She is pressed by her uncle and cousin to marry him, forced to accept the friendship of his sister, even sent back to Portsmouth in order that the pressures of poverty might bring her to her senses. Before *she* can yield, Henry Crawford himself yields to the temptation of seducing Maria, and leaves Fanny justified in her opinions and actions. The moral weaknesses of the other characters are revealed, the dangers of education without real concern for principle are exposed, and humility is justified.

The book, then, centres round Fanny, though she is not the centre of the action at least in the first part—her social position is too insignificant, her character too timid, her constitution too sickly for her to be active. At first she is static and observant, while the others take up the action around her. In the second part she is forced into prominence, and action centres on her.

The novel concludes, as usual, with seduction and elopement removed to a distance—viewed more seriously here and with more lasting consequences than in the other novels—and the removal into irony of the author:

> I purposely abstain from dates on this occasion, that every one may be at liberty to fix their own, aware that the cure of

unconquerable passions, and the transfer of unchanging attachments, must vary much as to time in different people.—I only
intreat every body to believe that exactly at the time when it was
quite natural that it should be so, and not a week earlier,
Edmund did cease to care about Miss Crawford, and became as
anxious to marry Fanny, as Fanny herself could desire.   *48, 470*

THE HEROINE

To many modern readers, the book's greatest weakness lies in
the character of the heroine. Fanny Price is a Cinderella figure,
and there is nothing wrong with that. Such a figure generally
draws the reader's sympathy. But Fanny has no energy, no
brilliance, no wit. She is like Elinor Dashwood in being always
right in her actions and judgements, but she lacks Elinor's
decisiveness and occasional irony. And, moreover, while Elinor
had sympathy for others, would see the best in them, was
'candid', Fanny seems to have no sympathy, can only condemn,
and then be proved right. Fanny refuses to take part in the
theatricals, yet she cannot help envying the others:

> Every body around her was gay and busy, prosperous and
> important, each had their object of interest, their part, their
> dress. . . . She alone was sad and insignificant; she had no share
> in any thing; she might go or stay. . . . She could almost think
> any thing would have been preferable to this. . . . But reflection
> brought better feelings . . . she could never have been easy in
> joining a scheme which . . . she must condemn altogether.
>
> *17, 159-160*

Fanny is righteous, but she is also envious, and she also suffers
from jealousy:

> She could not feel that she had done wrong herself. . . . Her
> heart and her judgement were equally against Edmund's decision;
> she could not acquit his unsteadiness; and his happiness under it
> made her wretched. She was full of jealousy and agitation. Miss
> Crawford came with looks of gaiety which seemed an insult,
> with friendly expressions towards herself which she could
> hardly answer calmly.   *17, 159*

The 'spirit of banter or air of levity' is most offensive to her, and her hatred for Mary grows steadily in the second part of the book: 'Her friends leading her astray for years! She is quite as likely to have led *them* astray. They have all, perhaps, been corrupting one another' (*44*, 424).

There is no reason why Jane Austen should not have written a strongly moral novel with a strongly moral and ultimately justified heroine which was successful as a novel, but she does not succeed here. All that made the earlier novels attractive in terms of comedy has disappeared; health, vitality, and wit have been handed over to the enemy. There is no danger of Fanny making the wrong judgements that Elizabeth Bennet makes. It is almost as though Jane Austen thought that a character as independent as Elizabeth must come to grief, and that the only hope of making correct moral judgements lay in an uncourageous, conforming Fanny.

THE CRAWFORDS

Jane Austen's portrait of the Crawfords is skilled. Obviously she intended from the outset to condemn them, yet she made them attractive, as she knew such people were attractive. It is only on later readings of the novel, when we are aware of the conclusion of the book, that we begin to see the flashiness and shallowness in the Crawfords from the beginning. At first we are impressed by their good looks, their wit, their vitality, their good nature. They seem to be all that was approved in Elizabeth —only later do we detect something of the Isabella Thorpe.

It is Mary Crawford who, when the play is being acted, turns to Fanny for sympathy and help, and then protects her from the anger of the others when she is attacked for refusing to take part in the theatricals. And Henry is genuinely in love with Fanny, and never ceases to regret losing her. Both the Crawfords appreciate Fanny's virtues.

But they *are* calculating—'Matrimony was her [Mary's] object, provided she could marry well, and having seen Mr. Bertram in town, she knew that objection could no more be made to his person than to his situation in life' (*4*, 42). Ironically, she gives up Tom, the eldest son who would inherit the estate, and falls in love with the second son, Edmund. And indeed, until she reveals a wrong attitude to her brother's elopement, it looks as though she and Edmund will marry—she will give up the pleasures of the town for the life of a country parson's wife, though Fanny can see no happiness for either of them in this.

The Crawfords are witty—but the groundwork of their wit is a cynicism impossible in her heroines. Henry observes: 'Nobody can think more highly of the matrimonial state than myself. I consider the blessing of a wife as most justly described in those discreet lines of the poet, "Heaven's *last* best gift" ' (*4*, 43). Yet he goes far in desiring this gift when he falls in love with Fanny, though there is in his protestations then, perhaps, too much of self-display. And when Mary says, apologising for monopolising Fanny's horse—

> 'My dear Miss Price . . . I am come to make my own apologies for keeping you waiting—but I have nothing in the world to say for myself—I knew it was very late, and that I was behaving extremely ill; and, therefore, if you please, you must forgive me. Selfishness must always be forgiven, you know, because there is no hope of a cure.'
> *7*, 68

—we recognise that she is being ironic, but that there is some truth in what she says of her own selfishness, and that she herself acknowledges it.

OTHER CHARACTERS

Mrs. Norris is perhaps Jane Austen's most unpleasant character. In the novel, she is strongly linked with the Christian theme, being the widow of a clergyman and pretending to be charitable, self-denying, frugal and principled. In fact she is a hypocrite in this, being a miser, completely uncharitable and a flatterer. There is nothing humorous about her failings, and we cannot laugh at her as we can at, say, Lady Catherine de Bourgh. She is a cross Fanny has to bear, and it is a further test of Fanny's Christianity that she is gentle and obedient to her aunt Norris.

Lady Bertram is more comic, but being, as a character, as unobtrusive in the novel as she must have been in real life, her comments are few and this strain of humour is not strong. In the moral scheme, she represents selfishness—complete and unaware of itself—and again is a foil to Fanny.

The two Misses Bertram are intended as further contrasts to Fanny, both being selfish, conceited, spoilt and used to having their own way. It is their nature and education which are tested at first by temptation and proved inadequate, and Fanny's nature and education—totally different—which are tested afterwards and proved sound.

In this novel there is no character apart from the heroine who is the representative of right feeling and judgement. Sir Thomas is regarded as this by the other characters, but he is proved wrong. Edmund has many virtues and is able at first to guide Fanny, but he also succumbs to temptation. And so we are left with a heroine who is also the representative of right, as was Elinor Dashwood, and as Anne Elliot is to be in *Persuasion*.

It is not easy to understand the sudden appearance of such a serious and sombre novel, but it may be that Jane Austen was trying her hand at a different mode, and may not have been entirely satisfied with the result. On the other hand, certain concerns that appear in this novel are fundamental to her thinking, and re-appear in other novels, especially in *Persuasion*.

Emma

Emma is as much a contrast to *Mansfield Park* as that novel is to *Pride and Prejudice*. It is an ironical comedy, and the heroine is as different as possible from Fanny Price. The whole story revolves round Emma, almost all the action is seen through her eyes and, as in *Pride and Prejudice* and *Northanger Abbey*, clues are scattered about which Emma misses or mis-interprets but which the reader can follow. Unlike *Pride and Prejudice* and *Sense and Sensibility* there is no division of two personality traits between two characters, no following out of this in the plot. True, Emma is blind to the truth of her own and others' situations, Mr. Knightley is not; Emma acts often without principle or on wrong principle, Mr. Knightley often points out to her her lack of principle, and himself embodies right principle; but this does not intrude into a division in the plot.

THE HEROINE

Jane Austen herself spoke of Emma as a 'heroine whom no one but myself will much like,' and indeed, many of Emma's characteristics and actions are so unpleasant as to make it difficult to know why one should like her.

Emma is like Elizabeth Elliot in situation and character: like Elizabeth she is of high social standing, and has also social importance; like Elizabeth, she has been mistress of her father's establishment for many years, though still a young woman; like Elizabeth, she is first among the women in her social set, she is able to take a protégée, she has considerable influence in the immediate affairs about her; and like Elizabeth, Emma is a snob—unconsciously but completely. Her upbringing has only enhanced her sense of superiority and certainty, and blinded her to her own deficiencies. Emma lacks 'candour'. Her likes and dislikes are strong and quickly made. She cannot admire Jane Fairfax however much she tries, she cannot but find Miss Bates a bore. Mr. Knightley, always urging a juster view on her, succeeds in making her try to do better, but Emma's nature is often intractable.

On the other hand, her vitality, her virtues as daughter and friend, her good nature and lack of vanity as to her personal beauty, to some extent account for our liking her. But what most endears Emma to us is her blindness—to see a brilliant, self-confident person, unaware of her own ignorance and naïveté, taking step after step into comic entanglements, gives us a feeling of superiority and yet allows us to sympathise.

THEMES AND STRUCTURE

It is impossible to discuss theme or structure without discussing Emma, who is both. The theme is announced through a description of the heroine's character at the start of the novel:

> Emma Woodhouse, handsome, clever, and rich, with a comfortable home and happy disposition, seemed to unite some of

the best blessings of existence; and had lived nearly twenty-one years in the world with very little to distress or vex her. . . .

The real evils . . . of Emma's situation were the power of having rather too much her own way, and a disposition to think a little too well of herself; these were the disadvantages which threatened alloy to her many enjoyments. The danger, however, was at present so unperceived, that they did not by any means rank as misfortunes with her.   *1*, 5-6

The structure of the novel leads from this, being a demonstration of how these weaknesses of Emma bring her into difficulties. Apart from Mr. Knightley's protests, Emma goes her way in a fog of flattery and approval from the rest of her world, until she is brought to an awareness at last of her own blindness:

With insufferable vanity had she believed herself in the secret of everybody's feelings; with unpardonable arrogance proposed to arrange everybody's destiny. She was proved to have been universally mistaken; and she had not quite done nothing—for she had done mischief. She had brought evil on Harriet, on herself, and she too much feared, on Mr. Knightley.   *47*, 412-413

THE PATH TO SELF-KNOWLEDGE—EMMA SELF-DECEIVED

Emma begins, then, with the classical situation of a person blinded by arrogance and conceit—in the nature of things, he or she must be brought low.

Emma, congratulating herself upon having arranged the Weston marriage, will now make one more match, this time for Mr. Elton, the vicar of Highbury.

Her next action is the adoption of Harriet Smith, whom she means to 'improve', though the real reason for her interest is to avoid boredom—'the evening no longer dreaded by the fair mistress of the mansion' since Harriet was to be there. Harriet's limitations are immediately apparent to the reader, though Emma can blind herself to them—'she must have good sense and deserve encouragement'. Adoption is one thing, direction of other people's lives another. Emma decides to make a match between Harriet and Mr. Elton, and then causes Harriet to reject a proposal of marriage from Robert Martin.

Emma is not all blindness—she can see from Robert Martin's letter that he is sensible, not coarse, but she cannot allow him to come between Harriet and her plans for Harriet. She can see that Mr. Elton is in love, but she wishes him to be in love with Harriet, and cannot see that he might be in love with herself. His proposal brings Emma's first moments of self-knowledge:

> The first error and the worst lay at her door. It was foolish, it was wrong, to take so active a part in bringing any two people together. It was adventuring too far, assuming too much, making light of what ought to be serious, a trick of what ought to be simple. She was quite concerned and ashamed, and resolved to do such things no more. *16*, 136-137

And the next moment she catches herself looking round for a second choice for Harriet!

Emma does face up to her mistakes—she does suffer for them. And Mr. Knightley never minces his words to her, which also helps her to gain our sympathy:

> 'Upon my word, Emma, to hear you abusing the reason you have, is almost enough to make me think so too. Better be without sense, than misapply it as you do.' *8*, 64

It is Emma's misfortune that her cleverness has no worthy opponent. Harriet can never stand up against her, as Emma's arguments against Robert Martin show. She sows the seeds of distrust as to Robert's nature: 'his being illiterate and coarse need not disturb *us*' (*4*, 34)—so he is damned without argument. She refuses to guide Harriet in her reply to his letter, yet forces her into refusal by assuming that nothing but a refusal is in mind:

> 'Your meaning must be unequivocal . . . and such expressions of gratitude and concern for the pain you are inflicting as propriety requires. . . .'
> 'Ought to refuse him! My dear Harriet, what do you mean? Are you in any doubt as to that? I thought—but I beg your pardon, perhaps I have been under a mistake.' *7*, 51-52

Emma needs to suffer later, needs to be made aware of her mistakes, if we are to forgive her for her treatment of Harriet, for such incidents as the morning call on the Martins, for such schemes as the breaking of her shoelace in Vicarage Lane.

EMMA DECEIVED BY OTHERS

Thus the first act ends. The second begins with the arrival of Jane Fairfax in Highbury, followed by Frank Churchill. Emma has given up match-making, but not for herself—she is prepared to consider Frank as a future husband, and at the same time she allows her imagination to form all kinds of disastrous alliances in Jane Fairfax's past. Again we have a fundamental disagreement between Mr. Knightley and Emma, showing him as having the correct opinion, and pointing to the irony of what follows:

> 'My idea of him [Frank Churchill] is, that he can adapt his conversation to the taste of every body, and has the power as well as the wish of being universally agreeable. To you, he will talk of farming; to me, of drawing or music; and so on to every body, having that general information on all subjects which will enable him to follow the lead, or take the lead, just as propriety may require, and to speak extremely well on each; that is my idea of him.'
>
> 'And mine', said Mr. Knightley warmly, 'is, that if he turn out any thing like it, he will be the most insufferable fellow breathing! What! at three-and-twenty to be the king of his company—the great man—the practised politician, who is to read every body's character, and make every body's talents conduce to the display of his own superiority. . . .'   *18,* 150

And to some extent it is true—Frank is a politician. To some extent, he uses Emma's inclination for him as a cloak for his feelings for and his relationship to Jane. At certain points, such as at Box Hill, he deliberately flirts with Emma to make Jane jealous. By that time, Emma is sure she is not in love with him, but she is still prepared to flirt with him. Carefully feeling out the situation first, he joins her in criticism of Jane, and encourages her fancies about Jane and Mr. Dixon. Again Emma, involved in a kind of imaginative curiosity about the world, is blind to the truth, and in this case becomes the dupe of Frank Churchill who uses her exactly as he wishes. He credits her with more perception than she has, even then, for when later he asks, 'But is it possible that you had no suspicion?—I mean of late. Early, I know you had none', her reply is, 'I never had the smallest, I assure you' (54, 477).

It is Emma's ironic fate that events should go against her in this way, and that while she is considering Frank as a husband, and Jane as crossed in love, she should be made his shield to conceal his intrigue with Jane. But there is a further complication. Resolved not to match-make, there is yet nothing to prevent Emma making matches in her mind, and she makes another for Harriet with Frank. Again she accepts unquestioningly her own valuation of the importance of an incident to another person. To Emma, the incident of Harriet being rescued from the gypsies by Frank is romantic enough to make it natural for Harriet to be in love with Frank. To Harriet, it is the slight she received from Mr. Elton at the ball that was the greater hurt, and Mr. Knightley's gentlemanly behaviour that aroused her devotion. When they discuss the incident they are therefore at cross-purposes.

> 'I am not at all surprised at you, Harriet. The service he rendered you was enough to warm your heart.'
> 'Service! oh! it was such an inexpressible obligation!—The very recollection of it, and all that I felt at the time—when I saw him coming—his noble look—and my wretchedness before. Such a change! In one moment such a change! From perfect misery to perfect happiness.'   40, 342

Harriet has a more sensitive appreciation than Emma gives her credit for. Thus even her puppet turns in her hand and takes on a life and understanding of its own.

Emma suffers and repents. After Mr. Knightley's scoldings, she does penance with Miss Bates. She tries to do penance with Jane Fairfax and is rejected. She finds her little protégée her rival in love. She lays herself open to be the dupe of others. Emma's sufferings are so great, her plight eventually so humiliating, that we must sympathise with her. And since it is a world of comedy, she will obtain Knightley, and Harriet will recover her lost love for Robert Martin and go to her proper place.

There is not the same ironic withdrawal at the end of the novel as there is in others—there is not the same speedy rejection. But the irony remains—as a comic irony. The difficulty that prevents Emma's wedding is her father's objection to marriages. It is got over in ironic fashion: 'Mrs. Weston's poultry-house was robbed one night of her turkies', and such a prosaic, non-romantic incident is to change Mr. Woodhouse's mind and make the marriage possible—Knightley becomes a necessity for Mr. Woodhouse's safety: 'He was very uneasy; and but for the sense of his son-in-law's protection, would have been under wretched alarm every night of his life. . . . But Mr. John Knightley must be in London again by the end of the first week in November. . . . The result of this distress was, that . . . [his daughter] was able to fix her wedding-day. . . .' (55, 483-484).

The conclusion of *Emma* reveals Jane Austen's own pleasure in her creation:

> 'But, in spite of these deficiencies, the wishes, the hopes, the confidence, the predictions of the small band of true friends who witnessed the ceremony, were fully answered in the perfect happiness of the union.'   55, 484

OTHER CHARACTERS

The other characters in the novel present perhaps the most convincing set of portraits of any of her novels. Each can be seen in relation to Emma's self-deception and self-approval.

It is important that the characters should all have lives and interests of their own to concern them of which Emma is ignorant. She is to see only the surface of their behaviour which misleads her—she can never penetrate beyond it to their true motives and actions. Thus, Miss Bates' flow of words disguises much of Jane Fairfax's true sufferings. Jane Fairfax effectively conceals her relationship with Frank Churchill, and Frank's flirtation with Emma and his apparently erratic behaviour also mislead Emma. Mr. Elton's interest in her, and Mr. Knightley's love for her, are both unobserved by Emma. At the same time, these concealed interests on the part of the other characters help to create a convincing world round the heroine.

On the other hand, Mr. Woodhouse is like Emma in that he also sees only a projection of his own interests around him—in this case, the interests of the hypochondriac.

Mrs. Elton is a kind of unpleasant reflection of Emma. She is conceited, self-important, a snob and social climber. She has married the man Emma rejected, and like Emma, she takes a protégée in the person of Jane Fairfax. Like Emma she is also deceived as to the true situation where her protégée is concerned.

In *Emma*, as in *Persuasion*, the male characters take on a certainty of presentation and life lacking in the heroes of earlier novels—Mr. John Knightley with his acerbity and uncertain temper; Mr. Knightley with his admiration for Emma, his generosity, his impatience of faults; Frank Churchill with his liveliness and love of intrigue, are all people in their own right.

Persuasion

Persuasion, published with *Northanger Abbey* after her death, provides some further surprises within the limits of Jane Austen's art. If *Emma* is the high-point of her comedy and celebrates the vital but deceived heroine, *Persuasion* marks her success in drawing the good, Cinderella heroine. But Anne Elliot is not simply a Cinderella. In many ways she is a new kind of heroine for Jane Austen. At the same time, the hardness and brilliance of *Emma* give way here to a sadder, warmer, autumnal atmosphere.

THEMES AND STRUCTURE

The structure of the novel is a simple one—it is concerned only to bring Anne Elliot and Captain Wentworth together. Like *Mansfield Park*, the novel falls into two sections. In the first, Anne, always in the background, is forced to witness Wentworth's courtship of Louisa Musgrove. In the second, the situation is reversed and Wentworth is witness to Mr. Elliot's courtship of Anne. The climax to the first part comes with Louisa Musgrove's accident on the Cobb at Lyme, an accident intended to show the disadvantages of a strong, determined mind, and also Anne's ability to take charge in a crisis. It is this accident which makes Wentworth realise that he still loves her. The climax of the second part comes with his overhearing Anne's spirited defence of woman's constancy in love, which persuades him that she might still love him.

The background to their love is formed by the contrast between the pride and superciliousness of the Elliots and the warmth and friendship and loyalty of Wentworth's sailor friends. The latter aspect grows in strength as Anne turns with more determination and less timidity towards Wentworth.

A major theme in the novel is pride and vanity—pride in one's social position, and vanity in one's personal appearance. The novel opens with the theme of pride in the character of Sir Walter Elliot, and in his eldest daughter Elizabeth. 'The Elliot pride' is seen also in Mary Elliot, and in his heir, Mr Elliot. It is a pride which rests on social distinctions and empty show. Even Lady Russell, the old friend of the family, is tainted by it.

And it is this pride which brings us to Anne Elliot's disappointment in love, which had occurred seven years before the novel opened. At nineteen, Anne had met Frederick Wentworth —she was then 'an extremely pretty girl, with gentleness, modesty, taste, and feeling', he was 'a remarkably fine young man, with a great deal of intelligence, spirit and brilliancy' (4, 26). They fell in love, but the match was opposed by her father and by Lady Russell on the grounds of Captain Wentworth's lack of social status, connections, future hopes, and fortune, on the grounds of class. It would be 'a degrading alliance' for Anne. Anne gives up the engagement, thinking she is consulting his good in doing this, but at twenty-seven she thinks differently: 'She had been forced into prudence in her youth, she learned romance as she grew older' (4, 30). She believes she ought to have continued the engagement.

This is the situation at the beginning of the novel. The Elliot pride prevents Sir Walter economising, and so forces him to rent out his home, Kellynch Hall, and take a house in Bath. His tenant is Admiral Croft, brother-in-law of Captain Wentworth. The Elliot pride which drove the lovers apart is now the means of bringing them together. But although they meet socially, another form of pride prevents any forgiveness on Captain Wentworth's part. He is rich, intends to marry—any girl but Anne Elliot. Angry pride is what now motivates him in attempting to find a wife, just as pride prevented him proposing to Anne once more when his fortunes improved. And it is inevitable that he should have in mind a woman opposite to Anne in not being timid or easily persuaded—someone with a strong mind.

But a further major concern of the novel is right quality of mind, which is bound up with the idea of persuadability. Captain Wentworth is convinced that Anne gave him up because she yielded too easily to persuasion. Anne, while aware that judgement on this cannot be absolute, concludes:

> 'I have been thinking over the past, and trying impartially to judge of the right and wrong, I mean with regard to myself; and I must believe . . . that I was perfectly right in being guided by [Lady Russell], . . . To me, she was in the place of a parent. . . . I am not saying that she did not err in her advice. It was, perhaps, one of those cases in which advice is good or bad only as the event decides. . . . But I mean, that I was right in submitting to her. . . I should have suffered more in continuing the engagement . . . because I should have suffered in my conscience . . . . and if I mistake not, a strong sense of duty is no bad part of a woman's portion.'   *23, 246*

The right balance is sought between the cold formality and calculation of the Elliots, and the instinctive intuitiveness of the Crofts in their marriage; between the impetuous, headstrong Louisa Musgrove, and the Anne Elliot of nineteen who yielded to persuasion. It involves an inquiry into the right balance between duty and principle and the satisfaction of personal whim and desire. Thus, when Mary and Charles leave Anne to look after their sick child while they go to dinner to meet Captain Wentworth she reflects: 'They were gone, she hoped, to be happy, however oddly constructed such happiness might seem' (*7, 58*), since personal desire had overcome parental love and duty. And when Captain Wentworth remarks to Louisa: 'It is the worst evil of too yielding and indecisive a character, that no influence over it can be depended on' (*10*, 88), he has Anne in mind. The novel goes on to prove that there is a middle state between this kind of persuadability, and the refusal to be persuaded. Firmness of character, as well as persuadability of temper, 'should have its proportions and limits' (*12*, 116).

And the proof of Anne's right character lies in her constancy in love. Captain Benwick's show of grief for his dead fiancée—ostentatious and poetic as it is—is very soon over, as is his love for her. Anne, with no show apart from the rejection of two possible husbands, continues to love Captain Wentworth when all hope of his loving her again has been given up.

The structure centres, therefore, on her growing towards a second beauty and happiness and confidence, and on Captain Wentworth's growing to forgiveness and acknowledgement of his love for her—two converging lines.

FAULTS OF STRUCTURE

The greatest fault in the structure of the novel is Mrs. Smith's narrative. We know that Jane Austen worked on the revision of the proposal scene between Anne and Wentworth, and improved the scene enormously. Perhaps her increasing illness prevented her from doing something about Mrs. Smith. Whereas Frank Churchill's letter in *Emma* is a necessary and fairly well-contrived account, Mrs. Smith's story is necessary, but clumsily contrived. Mrs. Smith, to begin with, is as characterless as her name, and her trials and tribulations under Mr. Elliot's persecution remind one too much of the eighteenth-century popular novel to be credible. Mr. Elliot is turned into a cardboard villain as a result.

THE HEROINE

Anne is unusual as a Jane Austen heroine, since she is older and more mature than the others. She is twenty-seven, and we remember that Marianne in *Sense and Sensibility* stated: 'A woman of seven and twenty . . . can never hope to feel or inspire affection again. . . .' (*5*, 38). And Elizabeth Elliot, at twenty-nine 'felt her approach to the years of danger' (*P. 1*, 7).

86

She is also unusual in that she embodies characteristics of both of Jane Austen's earlier types of heroine—she is a kind of final conclusion on Jane's part as to the nature of women. She is a Cinderella, like Fanny Price. She 'was only Anne', rejected, ignored, pushed into the background. Like Fanny and Elinor Dashwood she must witness her lover becoming involved with another woman, like them she has 'candour' and right judgement. Yet she is not self-righteous, we have no inclination to dislike her, we can sympathise with her.

Anne's judgements are correct because they are the outcome of earlier experience, and experience which has involved her in much personal suffering. Moreover, although she is ignored, she does not sit there feeling sorry for herself. Seeing Wentworth courting Louisa, she does not lack sympathy for her rival. She can acknowledge her merits, and acknowledge also that she herself, with faded looks and a retiring nature, is no match for her. But she can make herself useful to others such as Captain Benwick, and she can take charge in a crisis. She has an outgoing sympathy and charity which in turn rouse the reader's sympathy. Anne has no arrogance, she is not a snob, she has no vanity either of intellect or social position or virtue. She has learned through suffering the true values of life and can appreciate them objectively, when she observes them in the sea-going community with which she is brought into contact. Anne has only one thing to learn—to have more confidence in herself, to acknowledge that she might yet arouse love. Except for this, she does not go through the educative process of the other heroines.

But Anne is like the more vital heroines in having her own quiet decision of character, her own independence of outlook and of choice, and an ability to express herself forcefully when the situation requires it.

> Anne was ashamed. Had Lady Dalrymple and her daughter even been very agreeable, she would still have been ashamed of the agitation they created, but they were nothing. There was no superiority of manner, accomplishment, or understanding .... and when Anne ventured to speak her opinion of them to Mr. Elliot, he agreed to their being nothing in themselves, but

still maintained that as a family connexion, as good company, as those who would collect good company around them, they had their value. Anne smiled and said,

'My idea of good company, Mr. Elliot, is the company of clever, well-informed people, who have a great deal of conversation; that is what I call good company.'   *16*, 149-150

In the second part of the novel she gains courage and confidence and goes forward to speak to Captain Wentworth at the concert; and in her conversation with Captain Harville at the White Hart she can express herself as vitally as Emma or Elizabeth Bennet.

Anne, like Fanny and Emma and Elizabeth, is the 'eye' of the novel—the events that take place are witnessed and commented upon by her, but she is not the misguided heroine treated ironically by fate, she is the heroine who judges rightly.

OTHER CHARACTERS

The characters fall into three groups—the Elliot group, the Musgroves, and the sea-faring group, and these groups demonstrate various aspects of the novel's concerns.

Snobbishness, pride, vanity, all appear in the Elliot group, together with flattery and deceit. Just as Mrs. Clay ingratiates herself by flattery with the Elliots, so the Elliots in turn ingratiate themselves with Lady Dalrymple. This is the obverse of the Elliot pride. Mr. Elliot, since he values such connections as the Dalrymples, reveals his worldliness. The sea-faring group are perhaps the most convincing minor characters Jane Austen ever drew, especially Admiral Croft, and as we have suggested, they represent vitality, good nature, friendship and loyalty. It is significant that there are no flatterers or sycophants among their community. The Musgroves stand between these groups, important only in that their family first comes between Anne and Wentworth, and is then instrumental, through the family party at the White Hart, in bringing them together again.

6

Marriage and Morals

'It is a truth universally acknowledged, that a single man in possession of a good fortune, must be in want of a wife.' This opening sentence of *Pride and Prejudice* could be taken as the theme of each of her six novels. In the first place it is a comically ironic statement—an attitude of mind characteristic of Jane Austen. What she is implying is that 'a single man in possession of a good fortune' must be the target of all the unmarried women about him who are looking for husbands.

But the ironic humour must not be allowed to disguise the fact that we have here the opening of a love story. The statement introduces the subject of the romantic novel, which is courtship and marriage. By the time we have reached the end of one of Jane Austen's novels, not only the hero and heroine but most of the other young people in the story have succeeded in pairing off in marriage. And it is from the courtship of the hero and heroine that the stories derive much of their tension. The question at the back of the reader's mind is always—Will Elizabeth marry Darcy? Will Edmund at last fall in love with Fanny? Will Anne win Captain Wentworth? One feels all the time that things must work out this way—our concern is, How will it all come about? Indeed for many people, the enjoyment obtained from reading the novels lies in the fact that she is telling a romantic story which includes some comedy. There is a danger here that the average female reader will take the romance at its face value, and that the average male reader will see only the conventional love story and despise it accordingly.

Marriage is the end of her novels, but it involves more than the conclusion of a simple love story. It was, of course, an important social concern of her time, and Jane Austen, in her letters to her niece, Fanny Knight, has expressed fairly fully her views on the subject. She never married herself, but she was one of a marrying family and the looker-on sees most of the game.

She was, as we have shown, fully aware of the disadvantages of remaining single: 'Single Women have a dreadful propensity for being poor—which is one very strong argument in favour of matrimony . . .' (letter to Fanny Knight). Miss Bates, we remember, 'enjoyed a most uncommon degree of popularity for a woman neither young, handsome, rich, *nor married*' (my italics). And it is this motive that is reflected by Charlotte when she is giving Elizabeth her reasons for accepting Mr. Collins:

> 'I am not romantic you know. I never was. I ask only a comfortable home; and considering Mr. Collins's character, connections, and situation in life, I am convinced that my chance of happiness with him is as fair, as most people can boast on entering the marriage state.'   PRIDE AND PREJUDICE *22, 125*

Charlotte, Jane Austen tells us bluntly, 'Without thinking highly either of men or of matrimony', had always had marriage as her object; 'it was the only honourable provision for well-educated young women of small fortune, and however uncertain of giving happiness, must be their pleasantest preservative from want' (*P. & P. 22,* 122-123).

Neither is Elizabeth romantic, but like most of Jane Austen's heroines, she has a certain ideal of marriage based on her observation of the marriages she knows—there is a certain curiosity about the way such things will work out. When they leave Rosings, she reflects:

> 'Poor Charlotte!—it was melancholy to leave her to such society!—But she had chosen it with her eyes open; and though evidently regretting that her visitors were to go, she did not seem to ask for compassion. Her home and her housekeeping, her parish and her poultry, and all their dependent concerns, had not yet lost their charms.'   PRIDE AND PREJUDICE *38, 216*

Considerations of rank and fortune can also enter into the arranging of a marriage. Lady Catherine de Bourgh puts the case plainly to Elizabeth:

> 'My daughter and my nephew are formed for each other. They are descended on the maternal side, from the same noble line; and, on the father's, from respectable, honourable, and ancient, though untitled families. Their fortune on both sides is splendid. They are destined for each other by the voice of every member of their respective houses. . . .' PRIDE AND PREJUDICE 56, 356

And Emma, while she is angry at Mr. Elton for rejecting Harriet on the grounds of social consequence and rank, is annoyed also that he should aspire *above himself to her*. And Mr. Elton *is* aware of rank:

> '*I* think seriously of Miss Smith! . . . Every body has their level: but as for myself, I am not, I think, quite so much at a loss. I need not so totally despair of an equal alliance, as to be addressing myself to Miss Smith!' EMMA *15*, 131-132

He goes off to find an 'equal alliance' in the charming Augusta Hawkins who, 'in addition to all the usual advantages of perfect beauty and merit, was in possession of an independent fortune, of so many thousands as would always be called ten . . .' (*22*, 181).

But passion, as opposed to calculation, can equally result in an ill-judged match. Mr. Bennet in *Pride and Prejudice* and Mr. Palmer in *Sense and Sensibility* are both men who made unsatisfactory marriages through being captivated by pretty faces that concealed empty heads. And Elizabeth reflects on her sister Lydia's marriage: 'But how little of permanent happiness could belong to a couple who were only brought together because their passions were stronger than their virtue, she could easily conjecture' (*P. & P. 50*, 312). These are hasty marriages entered into for the wrong reasons, which result in uneasiness or compromise.

Writing to her niece, Jane Austen advised: 'Do not be in a hurry; depend upon it, the right Man will come at last; you will in the course of the next two or three years, meet with somebody more generally unexceptionable than anyone you have yet known, who will love you as warmly as ever *He* did, and who will . . . completely attach you. . . .' Marriage, then, ideally, is a love-match, and, still ideally, more is involved—the character and fortune of the lover:

> There *are* such beings in the World perhaps, one in a Thousand, as the Creature You and I should think perfection, Where Grace & Spirit are united to Worth, where the Manners are equal to the Heart & Understanding, but such a person may not come in your way, or if he does, he may not be the eldest son of a Man of Fortune, the Brother of your particular friend, & belonging to your own County.—Think of all this Fanny. Mr. J. P— has advantages which do not often meet in one person. His only fault indeed seems Modesty.

This attitude to marriage in her letters appears also in her novels. Jane Austen's heroines, though they may not always marry first sons of men of fortune, generally are able to attach themselves to men in whom 'Grace & Spirit are united to Worth, where Manners are equal to the Heart & Understanding'. And they usually have sufficient to live on comfortably.

The monetary aspect puzzles Elizabeth, or so she pretends:

> 'Pray, my dear aunt, what is the difference in matrimonial affairs, between the mercenary and the prudent motive? Where does discretion end, and avarice begin? Last Christmas you were afraid of his marrying me, because it would be imprudent, and now, because he is trying to get a girl with only ten thousand pounds, you want to find out that he is mercenary.'
>
> PRIDE AND PREJUDICE 27, 153

While protesting that wealth has nothing to do with happiness, the romantic Marianne cannot see herself supporting an establishment on less than a 'competence' of two thousand a year, while the sensible Elinor would be able to contemplate happiness on one thousand.

But to do her heroines—even Emma—justice, we must conclude that they all marry for love, and not for other considerations. As to the social and monetary aspects of their marriages, Jane Austen, in true romantic fashion, makes them 'all right'. Just as Elizabeth Bennet first rejects Darcy's proposal,

o Emma mentally rules out Frank Churchill. In both instances
these decisions are made on the grounds of incompatibility of
character and lack of attraction. In Elizabeth's case, it also
allows us to accept, unquestioningly, her later marriage to
Darcy and grant her the addition—as simply an accidental
bounty—of Pemberley's acres of parkland and the consequence
of being Mrs. Darcy, the mistress of them.

THE MARRIAGE OF TRUE MINDS

Jane Austen is not very optimistic on the subject of marriage—
it is rarely that we see a completely happy marriage in her
novels until the hero and heroine marry. Even in *Persuasion*
which presents more examples of at least comfortable partner-
ships than her other novels, we have the comment: 'With the
exception, perhaps, of Admiral and Mrs. Croft, who seemed
particularly attached and happy, (Anne could allow no other
exception even among the married couples). . . ' (*8*, 63).

But happy marriages do figure and do take place in Jane
Austen's novels. The right people do come together. And when
they do, the marriage that results involves a mutual process of
balancing each other's traits between the partners.

Elizabeth's realisation of Darcy's qualities shows Jane
Austen's belief in marriage based upon rightness of character:

> She began now to comprehend that he was exactly the man,
> who, in disposition and talents, would most suit her. His under-
> standing and temper, though unlike her own, would have
> answered all her wishes. It was an union that must have been to
> the advantage of both; by her ease and liveliness, his mind might
> have been softened, his manners improved, and from his judge-
> ment, information, and knowledge of the world, she must have
> received benefit of greater importance.
>
> PRIDE AND PREJUDICE *50*, 312

It would be a marriage to 'teach the admiring multitude what
connubial felicity really was.'

Marriage, then, is the concern of all her novels—right
marriage and wrong marriage, the right and wrong reasons for
marrying. As each novel shows, the good marriage depends

upon chance. So often, the hero and heroine almost do not come together, and there are generally two sets of objections which militate against the good marriage coming about.

The first objections are what we might call worldly—the intervention of friends, the inequality of position, the presence of another and superficially more attractive mate (Mary Crawford, Louisa Musgrove, Mr. Elliot, etc.).

The second objections are character traits which have to be altered before the hero and heroine can come together. Sensibility or pride has to be overcome, Emma has to rid herself of her blindness, Captain Wentworth has to recognise the requirements of his own heart. It is upon these two sets of circumstances that the tension in a Jane Austen novel depends. But the character traits which prevent the couple coming together are the more important because they affect judgement, and judgement is closely related to Jane Austen's moral view of the world.

THE IMPORTANCE OF CORRECT JUDGEMENT

In Jane Austen's novels people are always being judged, and such judgement involves the character of the judge. To form a right judgement, one must have right principles, and right perception of the nature of other people. One must be able to see through affectation, deception and hypocrisy; one must not be a victim of flattery; one must not make hasty decisions; and one must not be carried away by the opinions of other people.

The difficulties are summed up by Elinor in *Sense and Sensibility*. Speaking of Marianne, Edward Ferrars remarks that he had 'always set her down as a lively girl' and Elinor replies:

> 'I have frequently detected myself in such kind of mistakes . . in a total misapprehension of character in some point or other; fancying people so much more gay or grave, or ingenious or stupid than they really are, and I can hardly tell why, or in what the deception originated. Sometimes one is guided by what they say of themselves, and very frequently by what other people say of them, without giving oneself time to deliberate and judge.'

17, 9.

94

This ability to judge correctly is particularly important to her heroines, for it is upon this ability that their choice of a suitable husband depends. Thus, Elizabeth Bennet, so certain of her judgement at all times, does not judge according to the objective facts and so judges wrongly where Darcy is concerned. Elizabeth is, to begin with, too assured of her own powers of correct judgement. 'One does not know what to think,' says Jane Bennet. 'I beg your pardon;—one knows exactly what to think,' replies Elizabeth (*P. & P. 17*, 86). Elizabeth is blinded by prejudice which almost loses her the man she comes to love, but once the true facts are known to her, she realises her mistake:

> 'How despicably have I acted!' she cried—'I, who have prided myself on my discernment!—I, who have valued myself on my abilities! who have often disdained the generous candour of my sister, and gratified my vanity, in useless or blameable distrust. . . . Had I been in love, I could not have been more wretchedly blind. But vanity, not love, has been my folly. . . . Till this moment, I never knew myself.' PRIDE AND PREJUDICE *36*, 208

Correct judgement is, therefore, extremely important in Jane Austen's world, for if the marriage of true minds is the ultimate good in her world, the coming together of the true minds depends upon their knowledge of themselves and each other.

THE MORAL BACKGROUND

The basis of Jane Austen's morality is self-knowledge; this is the keystone of her beliefs: 'The knowledge of ourselves and our duty', as Edmund puts it in *Mansfield Park*. Jane Austen's outlook was of the eighteenth century, and therefore neat and well worked out. There *is* a basis for judgement and action, and there *are* standards by which one can live, and by abiding by them one can live happily. Not everyone, however, *can* live by them, not everyone *wants* to, not everyone *is able* to.

Mansfield Park, though probably one of her least successful novels, reveals her moral preoccupations most clearly, perhaps because the irony and humour of her other novels are not there to obscure the issues. Fanny Price, the timid but eventually justified heroine, clearly represents what, in theory at least, Jane Austen approved of. She stands out against theatricals, against the Crawfords, against Sir Thomas Bertram himself. The Crawfords are able to deceive even the most sound moral characters in the book such as Edmund and Sir Thomas, but not Fanny. Fanny always judges people correctly, and the Crawfords are eventually rejected totally—Why?

THE CASE OF 'MANSFIELD PARK'

The kindness shown to her by Mary cannot overcome Fanny's disapproval of her, nor can Henry's wooing of Fanny overcome her fundamental dislike of him. The reasons for this eventually appear. Mary had become suspect by voicing opinions on marriage, money and the clergy which were not acceptable. Henry had deliberately made Maria fall in love with him, and then deserted her. These are manifestations of moral weakness.

Speaking of Mary, Edmund eventually concludes:

> 'No, her's is not a cruel nature. I do not consider her as meaning to wound my feelings. The evil lies yet deeper; in her total ignorance, unsuspiciousness of there being such feelings, in a perversion of mind which made it natural to her to treat the subject as she did. . . . Her's are not faults of temper. . . . Her's are faults of principle, Fanny, of blunted delicacy and a corrupted, vitiated mind.'   MANSFIELD PARK *47*, 456

And Fanny's objections to Henry are:

> 'It is not merely in *temper* that I consider him as totally unsuited to myself . . . there is something in him which I object to still more. I must say, cousin, that I cannot approve his character.'
> *35*, 349

The distinction being made in both cases is between 'temper' or natural disposition, and 'character' (which Jane Austen sometimes calls disposition) which is composed of principles, judgement, and habits of thinking.

This then is the moral view of character that Jane Austen is concerned with—the temper, or natural bent, what we might call the nature of a person, and the character, formed of principles, judgement, good sense and self-knowledge. One may be taken in by the *temper* of a Mary Crawford, by her personality, but if the *character* is faulty it must be revealed eventually.

But this makes judgement difficult, especially since the revelation of the true character of a person may be delayed or may need to be changed and so add to the complications of the plot, the danger of the heroine failing to make a true marriage. Anne Elliot is fully aware of this difficulty of judging between the appearance a person wishes to give and his true character. Of Mr. Elliot she concludes:

> Though they had now been acquainted a month, she could not be satisfied that she really knew his character. . . that he talked well, professed good opinions, seemed to judge properly and as a man of principle,—this was all clear enough. He certainly knew what was right, nor could she fix on any one article of moral duty evidently transgressed; but yet she would have been afraid to answer for his conduct . . . who could answer for the true sentiments of a clever, cautious man, grown old enough to appreciate a fair character?' PERSUASION *17*, 160-161

Jane Austen's villains are generally dangerous because they can present a fair and deceiving front—Willoughby, Wickham and even Frank Churchill are deceivers in this respect.

THE EDUCATIVE PROCESS

Except in the case of Elinor Dashwood and Fanny Price, Jane Austen's heroines have to undergo a process of education, of enlightenment, before they can make correct judgements and marry the man of their choice. Similarly, her heroes undergo the same process. By this means, their characters are re-established on right principles, and their judgements corrected.

Marianne Dashwood, at the beginning of *Sense and Sensibility*, declares: 'I could not be happy with a man whose taste did not in every point coincide with my own. He must enter into all my feelings; the same books, the same music must charm us both' (*3*, 17). And in Willoughby, she finds such a man, but because her judgement is flawed, she cannot see that he is deceiving her. She learns eventually, not only that her happiness was never

Willoughby's object, but that her behaviour generally had been at fault: '. . . my own behaviour . . . nothing but a series of imprudence towards myself, and want of kindness to others' (*46*, 345). And so, at the end of the novel, Jane Austen's voice enters, underlying the change of outlook that has taken place:

> Marianne Dashwood was born to an extraordinary fate. She was born to discover the falsehood of her own opinions, and to counteract, by her conduct, her most favourite maxims. *50*, 378

After making marriages for everyone she encounters, but insisting on remaining single herself, it is the work of a moment for Emma to learn her final lesson of the novel:

> A few minutes were sufficient for making her acquainted with her own heart. . . . It darted through her, with the speed of an arrow, that Mr. Knightley must marry no one but herself!
> EMMA, *47*, 407-408

> How to understand the deceptions she had been thus practising on herself, and living under!—The blunders, the blindness of her own head and heart! . . . she had acted most weakly . . . she had been imposed on by others in a most mortifying degree . . . she had been imposing on herself in a degree yet more mortifying. . . . To understand, thoroughly understand her own heart, was the first endeavour. *47*, 411-412

THE FAILURE OF EDUCATION

Character is formed by upbringing and education, and many of Jane Austen's characters who fail in principle and judgement have had a faulty education. The effect of the Admiral's way of life on the Crawfords' upbringing is referred to many times— 'Henry Crawford, ruined by early independence and bad domestic example' (*M. P. 48*, 467). Sir Thomas realises the faults in his daughters' education:

> He feared that principle, active principle, had been wanting, that they had never been properly taught to govern their inclinations and tempers, by that sense of duty which can alone suffice. . . . He had meant them to be good, but his cares had been directed to the understanding and manners, not the disposition . . . he had

brought up his daughters, without their understanding their first duties, or his being acquainted with their character and temper.

48, 463-464

This failing is revealed dramatically during the visit to Sotherton when Julia Bertram is cut off from the other young people—and therefore from amusement—by being forced to walk with Mrs Rushworth and her aunt:

> Poor Julia, the only one out of the nine not tolerably satisfied with their lot, was now in a state of complete penance. . . . The politeness which she had been brought up to practise as a duty, made it impossible for her to escape [from Mrs. Rushworth and Mrs. Norris]; while the want of that higher species of self-command, that just consideration of others, that knowledge of her own heart, that principle of right which had not formed any essential part of her education, made her miserable under it. *9*, 91

It is this 'higher species of self command . . . knowledge of her own heart. . . . principle of right' that Anne Elliot has and which allows her, when in a similarly unhappy position, to remain tolerably happy. Often the process of education is doubled. A faulty education in youth results in those faults which the educative process of the novel corrects. Thus, Darcy admits that his pride was the fault of his upbringing—as a child he was encouraged to think a great deal of himself—but the events of the novel rid him of this pride.

Certain characters of Jane Austen's are not capable of improving or of degenerating. They are 'fixed', unaware of greater issues—Mrs. Allen, Lady Bertram, Miss Bates, Harriet, Mr. Collins. And as such they are unobnoxious, often figures of fun. But there are others who, while aware of other standards, either cannot attain them or attain them too late. Mr. Bennet and Sir Thomas Bertram are eventually aware that they have failed as fathers. Sir Thomas, as a result, is pleased to welcome Fanny as a daughter—'Sick of ambitious and mercenary connections, prizing more and more the sterling good of principle and temper . . .' (*M. P. 48*, 471). Mr. Bennet, typically, can be humorous over the whole business, and retire to his study without a thought in the world of doing anything serious about the situation in the future:

> 'No, Kitty, I have at last learnt to be cautious, and you will feel the effects of it. No officer is ever to enter my house again, nor even to pass through the village. Balls will be absolutely prohibited, unless you stand up with one of your sisters. And you are never to stir out of doors, till you can prove, that you have spent ten minutes of every day in a rational manner.'
>
> Kitty, who took all these threats in a serious light, began to cry.
>
> 'Well, well,' said he, 'do not make yourself unhappy. If you are a good girl for the next ten years, I will take you to a review at the end of them.' PRIDE AND PREJUDICE *48*, 300

But there are other characters, such as the Crawfords, who, while they drift towards a better morality, eventually reject it.

FOLLY AND VICE

Jane Austen distinguishes quite firmly between folly and vice in her moral scheme. Elizabeth Bennet admits that 'follies and nonsense' divert her; and towards the end of *Mansfield Park*, writing of Maria's affair with Henry Crawford and Julia's elopement with Yates, Jane Austen concludes: 'Maria's guilt had induced Julia's folly' (*48*, 467); and earlier, 'though Julia was yet as more pardonable than Maria as folly than vice' (*47*, 452). Edmund's illusions about Mary Crawford are finally shattered by the fact that she regards Maria's *guilt* merely as 'folly' (*47*, 455). In *Mansfield Park*, Julia is allowed to marry and remain acceptable, whereas Maria's vice condemns her to isolation with Mrs. Norris.

Vice for Jane Austen, perhaps because of the morals of her age, the conventions of the novel, or her own life, involves transgression of the sexual code. Her villains are all men who live loosely and seduce women, and her women who fall transgress the sexual code. Willoughby has already ruined Colonel Brandon's ward before he goes on to play with Marianne's feelings; Wickham has almost succeeded in seducing Darcy's sister before he elopes with Lydia; Henry Crawford first trifles with the affections of the Bertram sisters and then takes Maria from her husband; Mr. Elliot, unable to marry Anne, sets up Mrs. Clay as his mistress.

The horror aroused by these incidents, the seriousness with which they are regarded, varies with the tone of the novel. In *Mansfield Park*, where the moral atmosphere is so thick as to be stifling, the elopement involves Fanny in all the feelings of horror—sickness, tremblings, etc. Judgement on the guilty pair—guilty, of course, of vice—is severe, punishment is unremitting. In *Persuasion*, the emphasis falls rather on Mr. Elliot's other failings of character, the main interest in the novel being Anne's happiness. In *Emma*, Frank Churchill is guilty only of deception through concealing his engagement, and in *Pride and Prejudice*, Wickham is persuaded to marry Lydia, and the two are actually received in the parental home.

But the essence of evil is sexual. True, a seducer is probably guilty of other sins—of deceit and dishonesty, necessarily. Wickham is in debt, a liar, and a gamester. Mr. Elliot is a hypocrite and ruthlessly cruel to his old friend Mrs. Smith. But the emphasis is on the *sexual wrong*.

Fortunately, perhaps, Jane Austen's novels do not hang upon such vice. It serves, generally, for a *dénouement*, a climax, a touchstone, through which people and incidents and behaviour can be finally seen in a clear light and the sheep sorted out from the goats. It becomes a convention, and indeed she can rarely deal with seduction or elopement other than melodramatically. The interest in the novels lies elsewhere, in the irony, the humour, the interplay of character and the more acceptable moral discrimination. The vice is always in the sub-plot, and folly and nonsense are much more to the forefront.

Thus the romantic pattern of the novels, based upon the events of courtship and concluding with marriage, is a vehicle for serious moral problems which arise from the relationships of one human being with another. The novels involve us in a consideration of education, character, judgement, and right action, and while these are not the whole concern of Jane Austen, they are an important concern.

101

7

Comedy

'Follies and nonsense, whims and inconsistencies' diverted Elizabeth Bennet, and the same may be said of Jane Austen. Her attitude to a real-life Mr. Collins would have been the same as Mr. Bennet's: ' "Can he be a sensible man, sir?" "No, my dear; I think not. I have great hopes of finding him quite the reverse" ' (*P. & P. 13*, 64). Jane Austen, in her letters and her novels, treats life not as tragedy, not sentimentally, but primarily as comedy, and it is this characteristic of seeing the inconsistencies and incongruities in life, the incongruity between a person's pretensions and his abilities, between his words and his actions, that makes her primarily a comic writer.

Thus, Mr. Collins is a comic figure—he is absurd, but an innocent. He is a toady, and so conscientious a toady—it is so much his object in life—that we do not find him unpleasant as we do Uriah Heep in *David Copperfield*. Mr. Collins is comic because of an inconsistency in his character which Mr. Bennet, with an insight similar to Jane's, perceives: 'There is a mixture of servility and self-importance in his letter, which promises well' (*P. & P. 13*, 64). Servility and self-importance are incompatible characteristics. Normally, a person who has one would not have the other, but Mr. Collins does, and the result is comic. He had 'a mixture of pride and obsequiousness, self-importance and humility'. His obsequiousness is chiefly revealed in his veneration for his patroness, Lady Catherine de Bourgh:

> . . . he had never in his life witnessed such behaviour in a person of rank [here we expect praise to follow, but true to Mr.Collins' foolishness, we are given contradictory terms]—such *affability* and *condescension* (my italics).
> 14, 66

Similarly, he can equate terms as contradictory as 'dignity' and 'humility': '. . . I consider the clerical office as equal in point of dignity with the highest rank in the kingdom—provided that a proper humility of behaviour is at the same time maintained' (*18, 97*). 'Proper humility' is revealed in his letter to Mr. Bennet: '. . . it shall be my *earnest endeavour* [to work well? to achieve much? No—] to *demean* myself with grateful respect towards her Ladyship' (my italics) (*13, 63*).

Of course, Mr. Collins also always chooses the long word and the circumlocutory phrase; he insists on flattering Lady Catherine on every occasion, even when she is miles away; he is pompous and foolish; and all this additionally makes him comic. But the fundamental comedy derives from the basic incongruity in his character.

Awareness of a person's overriding sense of his own self-importance is another source of the comic for Jane Austen. Mary Elliot is always imagining herself ill, which is her means of increasing her self-importance:

> 'I am sorry to say that I am very far from well; and Jemima has just told me that the butcher says there is a bad sore-throat very much about. I dare say I shall catch it; and my sore-throats, you know, are always worse than anybody's.' PERSUASION *18*, 164

Lady Catherine de Bourgh is also given to self-praise, though of the more straightforward kind:

> There are few people in England, I suppose, who have more true enjoyment of music than myself, or a better natural taste. If I had ever learnt, [of course, she did not] I should have been a great proficient. PRIDE AND PREJUDICE *31*, 173

IRONY

A. An Attitude to People

Jane Austen's habit of not accepting the impression a person wishes to give of himself, but of always pointing to the truth that lies beneath the surface, is the attitude of irony. She is constantly ironic, so that her novels are like photographs in which the subject has moved and we have one likeness with another likeness just behind. But the second likeness, in this case, reverses the first. The contrast between the two gives rise to comedy, and implies also a critical view of life, because it shows where people are being pretentious, or dishonest, or absurd. Very rarely does Jane Austen give us a snapshot which has not a double image. Mrs. Smith in *Persuasion* is one of the few characters who can be taken straight:

> Anne found in Mrs. Smith the good sense and agreeable manners which she had almost ventured to depend on, and a disposition to converse and be cheerful beyond her expectation. Neither the dissipations of the past . . . nor the restrictions of the present; neither sickness nor sorrow seemed to have closed her heart or ruined her spirits. *17*, 153

This is surprising for Jane Austen. Mrs. Smith has all the virtues, and we are to accept them at their face value—Mrs. Smith has no pretensions and no incongruities.

Consider now, the following: 'Miss Bingley's congratulations to her brother, on his approaching marriage, were all that was affectionate and *insincere*' (my italics) (*P. & P. 60*, 383). Given the relationship of brother and sister, we naturally expect the congratulations to be affectionate and *sincere*. But Jane, aware of Miss Bingley's true nature, shows that her affection is insincere—she has penetrated Miss Bingley's pretences, she has given us a double image, and Miss Bingley is shown in her true colours. It is the placing together of the pretence and the truth that provides the ironic vision.

Simple irony is a statement that implies the opposite of what it is saying, or implies more than it is saying. In the following example, much more is implied than the surface meaning: 'Lady Lucas was enquiring of Maria across the table, after the *welfare* and *poultry* of her eldest daughter' (my italics) (*P. & P. 39*, 222). The placing together of these two divergent topics reveals the equality of interest they hold in Lady Lucas' mind. This method of making an ironic implication by means of the unexpected contrast, is used again in the following statement: 'Miss Lucas . . . accepted him solely from the *pure* and *disinterested* desire [this sounds very moral and proper until we reach the nature of the desire] of an *establishment*' (my italics) (*P. & P. 22, 122*). And the final clause of the following quotation, giving the true reason for Bingley's sisters' 'affection and solicitude' for Jane, reveals the hollowness of their intentions, again by contrasting the pretended with the actual:

> When breakfast was over, they were joined by the sisters; and Elizabeth began to like them herself, when she saw how much affection and solicitude they shewed for Jane . . . Elizabeth did not quit her room for a moment, nor were the other ladies often absent; the gentlemen being out, *they had in fact nothing to do elsewhere.* (my italics)
>
> PRIDE AND PREJUDICE *7*, 33

The technique of ironic statement frees Jane Austen from the necessity of making involved commentaries on her characters. It is left to the reader to understand the full force of the irony, and to make the criticism himself. Mr. Collins, for example, looking for a bride and being warned off Jane Bennet, switches to her sister: 'Mr. Collins had only to change from Jane to Elizabeth—and it was soon done—done while Mrs. Bennet was stirring the fire' (*P. & P. 15*, 71). Taken at its face value this is merely a statement of fact—while Mrs. Bennett stirred the fire, Mr. Collins decided to marry Elizabeth instead of Jane. But there are implications behind Jane Austen's statement brought out by phrases such as 'had only to change', 'soon done'. Mr. Collins is considering a serious step, i.e. marriage, yet the woman involved is of so little importance to him as a person that he can change his mind in a second. And as yet he knows nothing of the feelings of either sister towards him. This is an aspect of Jane Austen's technique of ironic comment—a statement which does not seem to involve the author in any judgement, but which illuminates a character without unnecessary comment.

But these ironic statements are all made by Jane Austen *about* her characters. A further technique of irony is to put a speech into a character's mouth which is not intended by the speaker as irony but becomes ironic in effect. In this case, *the character* is made to say more than he intends, though it is left to the reader to notice the implications.

On Lydia's elopement with Wickham, Mr. Collins writes to Mr. Bennet:

> I must not, however, neglect the duties of my station, or refrain from declaring my amazement, at hearing that you received the young couple into your house as soon as they were married. It was an encouragement of vice; and had I been the rector of Longbourn, I should very strenuously have opposed it. You ought certainly to forgive them as a christian, but never to admit them in your sight, or allow their names to be mentioned in your hearing. PRIDE AND PREJUDICE *57*, 363–364

It is left to the reader to reflect upon the deficiencies of Mr. Collins' Christianity.

The description of Mrs. Dashwood's process of rationalisation in *Sense and Sensibility* is a brilliant piece of irony. We are witness to Mrs. Dashwood gradually arguing her mother-in-law out of any material assistance from her son, with no intrusive comments from the author, to the final conclusion that the widow and her daughters will 'be much more able to give *you* [their wealthy step-brother] something':

> 'The assistance he [your father] thought of, I dare say, was only such as might be reasonably expected of you; for instance, such as looking out for a comfortable small house for them, helping them to move their things, and sending them presents of fish and game, and so forth, whenever they are in season. . . . They will live so cheap! Their housekeeping will be nothing at all. They will have no carriage, no horses, and hardly any servants; they will keep no company. . . . They will be much more able to give *you* something.' 2, 12

Similarly, when Elizabeth says to Anne, who has warned her that Mrs. Clay might have designs on Sir Walter—

> '. . . as I am rather better acquainted with her sentiments than you can be, I can assure you, that upon the subject of marriage they

are particularly nice; and that she reprobates all inequality of condition and rank more strongly than most people.'

PERSUASION 5, 35

—the reader, who has seen Mrs. Clay through other eyes and knows her better, acknowledges immediately that Mrs. Clay has had so much success. The propaganda she has put out has been accepted by Elizabeth who is then lulled away from any suspicions of her friend. The speech becomes ironic at Elizabeth's expense, revealing her as the dupe of Mrs. Clay whom she is defending.

B. *An Attitude to Life*

Thus we come to Jane Austen's ultimate ironic vision—that life itself is ironic. Expecting a certain result we bend all our efforts towards it, and find suddenly that the reverse of what we expected has come to pass. This view of life affects her novels since, very often, the plot itself has this ironic aspect of turning back on itself, so that the characters in her novels are forced into a similar reversal.

Emma Woodhouse, who prides herself on her match-making ability, is so involved in bringing about a marriage between Harriet and Mr. Elton, that she sees every circumstance as leading towards that end. She does not see that every event could just as easily be shown as evidence of Mr. Elton's love for herself. Thus Mr. Elton's unexpected proposal is an ironic reversal of her expectations, an irony which the reader fully appreciates since he has been expecting it all the time. And Emma is the dupe of circumstances not only in the case of Mr. Elton, Harriet, Jane Fairfax and Frank Churchill, but also where her own feelings for Mr. Knightley are concerned.

A necessary part of this irony is that the reader should have more knowledge of what is happening than the characters involved. So he watches them moving forward blindly, and can anticipate the shock they are to receive. We recognise that Elizabeth Bennet's claims to right judgement are invalidated by her prejudice against Darcy. Ironically, life is to show her how wrong she was.

Such irony is also apparent in *Northanger Abbey* where it depends upon the reader's knowledge of Gothic and sentimental fiction. Only a reader familiar with such fiction experiences the full force of the incident of the mysterious chest and the difficulty Catherine has in lifting its lid, only to find that it is of use 'in holding hats and bonnets' (*21, 165*); or realises that Catherine expects to read the story of some former maltreated heroine when she finds the roll of papers in the cabinet:

> Her greedy eye glanced rapidly over a page. She started at its import. Could it be possible . . . ? An inventory of linen, in coarse and modern characters, seemed all that was before her! If the evidence of sight might be trusted, she held a washing-bill in her hand.   *22, 172*

She has finally to conclude:

> Charming as were all Mrs. Radcliffe's works . . . it was not in them perhaps that human nature, at least in the midland counties of England, was to be looked for. Of the Alps and Pyrenees, with their pine forests and their vices, they might give a faithful delineation; and Italy, Switzerland, and the South of France, might be as fruitful in horrors as they were there represented. Catherine dared not doubt beyond her own country. . . .
> *25, 200*

But Jane Austen has a further irony in view for the reader in this novel, for her plot reveals that real life—the thing that Catherine had moved away from—can be every bit as disturbing as the events of a horror novel, and a girl who is patently not a heroine can, in her own small circle, become one. Deceit, mercenary motives, unconsidered rudeness can be as alarming and upsetting as murder, poison, imprisonment, and ghosts, and an ordinary girl can become the centre of a romance. And having demonstrated her own moral viewpoint throughout the whole tale, Jane Austen ends with a further irony—a tilt at the carefully drawn moral of the conventional novel:

> . . . I leave it to be settled by whomsoever it may concern, whether the tendency of this work be altogether to recommend parental tyranny, or reward filial disobedience.   *31, 252*

Frequently her general statements, which appear to be serious moral comments, are ironic. 'On every formal visit a child ought to be of the party, by way of provision for discourse' (*S. & S.* 6, 31) is not to be taken as a serious recommendation. It is an ironic reflection on the insipidity of social intercourse and the boring habits of parents who *will* talk about their children. Jane Austen goes on to show what she means by the statement:

> 'In the present case it took up ten minutes to determine whether the boy were most like his father or mother, and in what particular he resembled either, for of course every body differed, and every body was astonished at the opinion of the others.'
>
> 6, 31

The irony here is twofold—she reveals how the child becomes a centre for conversation and at the same time how ridiculous such conversation is.

Again:

> To be disgraced in the eye of the world, to wear the appearance of infamy while her heart is all purity, her actions all innocence, and the misconduct of another the true source of her debasement, is one of those circumstances which peculiarly belong to the heroine's life. . . .   NORTHANGER ABBEY 8, 53

Here we have the high-sounding, solemn language of morality—'infamy' 'purity' 'innocence'—used with ironic humour, for Jane Austen first applies it only to the life of the 'heroine'—a person she is likely to make fun of anyway. But the further irony is that this is all applied to a trivial incident—Catherine Morland, engaged to dance by John Thorpe, is left among the chaperons when her escort does not appear.

IRONY AND CRITICISM

The ironic view of life can be tragic. The Mayor of Casterbridge, Oedipus, and Macbeth are all in the hands of a fate which deals ironically with them, and the end is tragic in each case. Jane Austen's irony is based on a comic view of life, and her irony raises a smile—an appreciative smile, a broad smile, sometimes a bitter smile. But the ironic view also generally carries overtones of criticism, since it is pointing at weaknesses in character and in life. And Jane Austen can be harshly critical of some faults and attitudes.

Mrs. John Dashwood, in *Sense and Sensibility*, finds Lady Middleton: '. . . one of the most charming women in the world! Lady Middleton was equally pleased with Mrs. Dashwood.' Then we are given the second image—the real reason for the pleasure which reveals the two women in all their limitations of feeling, limitations which prevent them finding happiness in people of a truer nature:

> There was a kind of cold hearted selfishness on both sides, which mutually attracted them; and they sympathised with each other in an insipid propriety of demeanour, and a general want of understanding.   SENSE AND SENSIBILITY *34*, 229

But Jane Austen's ironic commentary on people and their motives and pretensions and failings does not carry with it a desire on her part to reform them. It is a gesture that is part humorous, part despairing. It implies on her side an acknowledgement of what is wrong with people and society and an acceptance of this as something one has to bear with and therefore might as well smile at. In this way it is similar to Mr. Bennet's irony.

Mr. Bennet, who has made a foolish marriage and finds himself caught up in the kind of life he wants no part of, surrounded by foolish daughters and foolish social conventions, cannot alter his situation or his society. He has only two means of defence— he can retire to his study and temporarily shut it all out, or he can indulge in an ironic humour at its expense which suggests an ironic resignation. Thus he can say: 'I admire all my three sons-in-law highly . . . Wickham, perhaps, is my favourite' (*P. & P. 59*, 379). And his reason has already been given: 'He is as fine a fellow . . . as ever I saw. He simpers, and smirks, and makes love to us all' (*53*, 330). And of course the reader is already fully acquainted with Wickham's true nature.

Similarly, Mr. Bennet takes some delight in pointing straight at Mr. Collins' subservience when he writes to him:

'Dear Sir,

'I must trouble you once more for congratulations. Elizabeth will soon be the wife of Mr. Darcy. Console Lady Catherine as well as you can. But, if I were you, I would stand by the nephew. *He has more to give. . . .*' (my italics)   *60*, 383

WIT

Jane Austen's major characters are often witty and it is from their perceptions and conversation that much humour arises. Elizabeth Bennet is constantly witty:

'I dare say [says Charlotte of Mr. Darcy] you will find him very agreeable.'

'Heaven forbid!—*That* would be the greatest misfortune of all!—To find a man agreeable whom one is determined to hate!—Do not wish me such an evil!'

PRIDE AND PREJUDICE *18*, 90

And her encounters with other characters give ample evidence of her quickness of mind:

'This is not to be borne. Miss Bennet, I insist on being satisfied. Has he, has my nephew, made you an offer of marriage?'

'Your ladyship has declared it to be impossible.'

'It ought to be so; it must be so, while he retains the use of his reason. But *your* arts and allurements may, in a moment of infatuation, have made him forget what he owes to himself and to all his family. You may have drawn him in.'

'If I have, I shall be the last person to confess it.'   *56*, 354

And to Mr. Darcy:

'. . . I have always seen a great similarity in the turn of our minds.—We are each of an unsocial, taciturn disposition, unwilling to speak, unless we expect to say something that will amaze the whole room, and be handed down to posterity with all the éclat of a proverb.'

'This is no very striking resemblance of your own character, I am sure,' he said. 'How near it may be to *mine*, I cannot pretend to say.—*You* think it a faithful portrait undoubtedly.'

'I must not decide on my own performance.'   *18*, 91

Emma also has a quick mind, and she is not averse to making fun of other characters by mimicking them:

> 'He is an excellent young man, and will suit Harriet exactly; it will be an "Exactly so", as he says himself . . .   EMMA 6, 49

> 'How would he bear to have Miss Bates belonging to him . . . thanking him all day long for his great kindness in marrying Jane?—"So very kind and obliging!—But he always had been such a very kind neighbour!" And then fly off, through half a sentence, to her mother's old petticoat. "Not that it was such a very old petticoat either—for still it would last a great while—and, indeed, she must thankfully say that their petticoats were all very strong."'   26, 225

COMEDY THROUGH MISUNDERSTANDING

Jane Austen has a quick ear for the minor embarrassments and the misunderstandings of social intercourse, and they also become a source of comedy. They are generally revealed through the dialogue since, for her, character is revealed in this way.

Mr. Bennet relies upon his wife's stupidity to supply him with amusement. She is invariably sent off on to a side issue by his ironic remarks, and never perceives his irony:

> 'I dare say Mr. Bingley will be very glad to see you; and I will send a few lines by you to assure him of my hearty consent to his marrying which ever he chuses of the girls; though I must throw in a good word for my little Lizzy.'
>
> 'I desire you will do no such thing. Lizzy is not a bit better than the others; and I am sure she is not half so handsome as Jane. . . .'   PRIDE AND PREJUDICE 1, 4

Mr. Bennet's suggested method of introducing his daughters to Mr. Bingley is, of course, as ironically comic as possible, but not only does Mrs. Bennet not observe the outrageousness of her husband's suggestion, but she also misses his humour. Instead, she takes up his comment about Elizabeth (in which he is being partially serious) and insists that he will not 'throw in a good word for Lizzie'. Thus, by implication, she takes his whole absurd suggestion as serious.

Some of the most comic moments in her novels appear when characters of limited outlook and fixed ideas attempt to converse with each other. Mr. Weston's concern with his son, Frank Churchill, and Mrs. Elton's pride in Maple Grove and sense of her own importance, make it impossible for them to listen to, let alone understand, each other:

'This letter tells us—it is a short letter—written in a hurry, merely to give us notice—it tells us that they are all coming up to town directly, on Mrs. Churchill's account—she has not been well the whole winter, and thinks Enscombe too cold for her—so they are all to move southward without loss of time.'

'Indeed!—from Yorkshire, I think. Enscombe is in Yorkshire?'

'Yes, they are about 190 miles from London. A considerable journey.'

'Yes, upon my word, very considerable. Sixty-five miles farther than from Maple Grove to London. But what is distance, Mr. Weston, to people of large fortune?—You would be amazed to hear how my brother, Mr. Suckling, sometimes flies about...'

'The evil of the distance from Enscombe,' said Mr. Weston, 'is, that Mrs. Churchill, *as we understand*, has not been able....'

EMMA *36*, 305-306

And for conversation between two unequals, we have only to turn to the inadequacies of comprehension between Mrs. Musgrove and Mrs. Croft in *Persuasion:*

'What a great traveller you must have been, ma'am!' said Mrs. Musgrove to Mrs. Croft.

'Pretty well, ma'am, in the fifteen years of my marriage; though many women have done more. I have crossed the Atlantic four times; and have been once to the East Indies, and back again; and only once, besides being in different places about home.... But I never went beyond the Streights—and never was in the West Indies. We do not call Bermuda or Bahama, you know, the West Indies.'

Mrs. Musgrove had not a word to say in dissent; she could not accuse herself of having ever called them any thing in the whole course of her life.

'... While we [she and her husband] were together, you know
there was nothing to be feared. . . . The only time that I eve
really suffered in mind or body . . . was the winter that I passe
by myself at Deal, when the Admiral (*Captain* Croft then) wa
in the North Seas. . . .'

'Ay, to be sure.—Yes, indeed, oh yes, I am quite of you
opinion, Mrs. Croft,' was Mrs. Musgrove's hearty answer. 'Ther
is nothing so bad as a separation. I am quite of your opinion
I know what it is, for Mr. Musgrove always attends the assizes
and I am so glad when they are over, and he is safe back again.

8, 70-7

But the supreme example of Jane Austen's ability to provid
comedy through characterization and without unnecessary com
mentary, is Mrs. Elton's monologue when, in all her 'apparatu
of happiness', she picks strawberries at Donwell Abbey. Th
monologue expresses not only Mrs. Elton's flagging beneath
the sun, but also the irritation of her unceasing commentary
and gives us some impression of the success of Mr. Knightley'
party (it is significant that on that morning also, Jane Fairfa
left Donwell in distress, and Frank Churchill arrived in irritation
Expeditions and explorations in Jane Austen's novels never turn
out well):

'The best fruit in England—every body's favourite—alway
wholesome.—These the finest beds and finest sorts.—Delightfu
to gather for one's self—the only way of really enjoying them.—
Morning decidedly the best time—never tired—every sort goo
—hautboy infinitely superior—no comparison—the other
hardly eatable—hautboys very scarce—Chili preferred—whit
wood finest flavour of all—price of strawberries in London—
abundance about Bristol—Maple Grove—cultivation—bed
when to be renewed—gardeners thinking exactly different—n
general rule—gardeners never to be put out of their way—
delicious fruit—only too rich to be eaten much of—inferior t
cherries—currants more refreshing—only objection to gathering
strawberries the stooping—glaring sun—tired to death—could
bear it no longer—must go and sit in the shade.'

EMMA *42*, 358-35

3

Character

THE CHARACTER SKETCH

Jane Austen's methods of drawing characters are in one respect remarkably straightforward. The basis of her character presentation is the character sketch. We have already mentioned her placing of the character in relation to society, which is part of his technique. The rest of the sketch is concerned with appearance, character, and the person's history. Scarcely any character —no matter how minor—is introduced without the preliminary sketch. Margaret Dashwood, youngest of the three Dashwood sisters in *Sense and Sensibility*, and with very little part in the plot, is nevertheless given the following introduction:

> Margaret, the other sister, was a good-humoured, well-disposed girl; but as she had already imbibed a good deal of Marianne's romance, without having much of her sense, she did not, at thirteen, bid fair to equal her sisters at a more advanced period of life.   *1, 7*

Sir Walter Elliot's character is firmly given in a few lines:

> Vanity was the beginning and the end of Sir Walter Elliot's character; vanity of person and of situation. He had been remarkably handsome in his youth; and, at fifty-four, was still a very fine man. . . . He considered the blessing of beauty as inferior only to the blessing of a baronetcy; and the Sir Walter Elliot, who united these gifts, was the constant object of his warmest respect and devotion.   PERSUASION *1, 4*

Emma Woodhouse is 'handsome, clever, and rich, with a comfortable home and happy disposition. . . . The real evils indeed of Emma's situation were the power of having rather too much her own way, and a disposition to think a little too well of herself. . . .' (*E. 1, 5*).

Alternatively, character may be presented more gradually through a variety of points of view. Fanny Price is seen initially only through the eyes of those around her. She is 'stupid' to her cousins and their governess; her 'tractable disposition' gives satisfaction to Mrs. Norris and Sir Thomas; she is useful to her aunt Bertram in running errands; only Edmund, who assists in the improvement of her mind, knows her 'to be clever, to have a quick apprehension as well as good sense, and a fondness for reading . . .' (*M. P. 2, 22*). Apart from this, she is good-natured, but timid and shy. Similarly, we are not fully acquainted with Anne Elliot's character until Chapter IV when it is drawn in relation to her unhappy engagement to Captain Wentworth. Elizabeth Bennet, Jane Austen's most striking heroine, is not given a character sketch. We form our opinion of her entirely from her speech and actions, and the remarks of such people as Mr. Darcy, her father, and Miss Bingley.

But in whatever way we learn of a character, that information forms a kind of logical proposition which is then proved by trying it out in a number of situations.

FIXED AND DEVELOPING CHARACTERS

Jane Austen has characters who do not change or develop within the novel, and may be called fixed. Others, generally the hero and heroine, do develop—they are 'educated', change their opinions, fall into error, etc. But whether fixed or developing, the formula is the same—first the basic description, or proposition, then its being tried out in a series of situations.

A fixed character will always react in the same way, whatever the situation. Mrs. Allen, for example, in *Northanger Abbey* has neither 'beauty, genius, accomplishment, nor manner.' She has the 'air of a gentlewoman', 'quiet, inactive good temper, and a trifling turn of mind'. 'Dress was her passion' (*2, 20*). Mrs. Allen never moves from these character traits. The crush in the

Assembly only arouses the fear that her gown might have been torn: 'It is such a delicate muslin.—For my part I have not seen any thing I like so well in the whole room' (*2,*22). She interrupts Catherine's conversation with Mr. Tilney with the request, '. . . do take this pin out of my sleeve; I am afraid it has torn a hole already; I shall be quite sorry if it has, for this is a favourite gown, though it cost but nine shilling a yard' (*3,* 28). When Catherine, anxious to visit the Tilneys to apologise for not meeting them for their walk, seeks her advice as to the propriety of calling on Miss Tilney, she advises: 'Go by all means, my dear; only put on a white gown; Miss Tilney always wears white' (*12,* 91). And when questioned on the propriety of young people driving about the country together in open carriages, she responds: 'Open carriages are nasty things. A clean gown is not five minutes wear in them' (*13,* 104). When told of Catherine's expulsion from Northanger Abbey, she repeats several times: 'I really have not patience with the General', but soon goes on: 'Only think, my dear, of my having got that frightful great rent in my best Mechlin so charmingly mended . . .' (*29,* 238).

'Vanity was the beginning and the end of Sir Walter Eliot's character; vanity of person and of situation', we are told. The navy being mentioned as a possible source for a tenant for Kellynch Hall, he immediately begins a lecture on the navy as cutting up 'a man's youth and vigour most horribly':

> 'One day last spring, in town, I was in company with two men, striking instances of what I am talking of: Lord St. Ives, whose father we all know to have been a country curate, without bread to eat; I was to give place to Lord St. Ives, and a certain Admiral Baldwin, the most deplorable looking personage you can imagine, his face the colour of mahogany, rough and rugged to the last degree, all lines and wrinkles, nine grey hairs of a side, and nothing but a dab of powder at top.—"In the name of heaven, who is that old fellow?" said I, to a friend of mine who was standing near (Sir Basil Morley). "Old fellow!" cried Sir Basil, "it is Admiral Baldwin. What do you take his age to be?" "Sixty," said I, "or perhaps sixty-two". "Forty," replied Sir

Basil, "forty, and no more". Picture to yourselves my amazement; I shall not easily forget Admiral Baldwin.'

PERSUASION *3*, 19-20

At Bath, he looks forward to meeting Mrs. Wallis:

> 'He hoped she might make some amends for the many very plain faces he was continually passing in the streets. The worst of Bath was, the number of its plain women. He did not mean to say that there were no pretty women, but the number of the plain was out of all proportion. He had frequently observed, as he walked, that one handsome face would be followed by thirty or five and thirty frights; and once, as he had stood in a shop in Bond-street, he had counted eighty-seven women go by, one after another, without there being a tolerable face among them.' *15*, 141–142

And he becomes reconciled to Anne's marriage to Captain Wentworth on the following grounds:

> Sir Walter indeed, though he had no affection for Anne, and no vanity flattered, to make him really happy on the occasion, was very far from thinking it a bad match for her. On the contrary, when he saw more of Captain Wentworth, saw him repeatedly by daylight and eyed him well, he was very much struck by his personal claims, and felt that his superiority of appearance might be not unfairly balanced against her superiority of rank. . . . *24*, 248

Such a formula does not apply in the same way to the developing characters, who, as we have shown, go through a process of enlightenment. But the principle is the same. Emma's self-importance and assurance must be tested in several situations, and always, until the end, her reaction is the same—she does not see the obvious. Elizabeth Bennet, proud of her discernment and judgement of character, is placed in one situation after another in which she must judge Darcy, and judges wrongly each time. Anne Elliot's lack of confidence in herself is tested in a variety of situations; Fanny Price's accuracy of judgement is similarly tried.

ane Austen's own acid comments are likely to determine our attitude to a character without our being fully aware of it. Thus Mr. Woodhouse's 'gentle selfishness'; Lady Middleton, initially handsome, her figure tall and striking, and her address graceful', in a few lines is damned: 'though perfectly well-bred, she was reserved, cold, and had nothing to say for herself beyond the most common-place inquiry or remark' (*S. & S. 6, 31*). Elizabeth Elliot is more strongly dismissed:

> Such were Elizabeth Elliot's sentiments and sensations; such the cares to alloy, the agitations to vary, the *sameness* and the elegance, the prosperity and the *nothingness*, of her scene of life. . . . (my italics). PERSUASION *1, 9*

Jane Austen does not hesitate to speak out, strongly and satirically, when it comes to revealing character faults. Not all such comments are the author's, of course, though there are times when it is difficult to know whether we are to lay a remark at her door, or at one of her characters':

> Elizabeth listened in silence, but was not convinced. . . . They [Bingley's sisters] were in fact very fine ladies; not deficient in good humour when they were pleased [which demerits their good humour immediately], nor in the power of being agreeable where they chose it [which credits them with a great deal of calculation]; but proud and conceited [which devaluates even the half-tones of the previous statements]. They were rather handsome, had been educated in one of the first private seminaries in town, had a fortune of twenty thousand pounds, were in the habit of spending more than they ought, and of associating with people of rank; and were therefore in every respect entitled to think well of themselves, and meanly of others [which, she is implying, is what they did, and on the grounds of money and snobbery]. PRIDE AND PREJUDICE *4, 15*

Clearly, either Jane Austen or Elizabeth Bennet or both did not like the Bingley sisters, yet Elizabeth can hardly have known them long enough to be acquainted with such details.

Obviously, characters do not exist in a vacuum. It is their reaction to other characters and to incidents that brings them to life; and confrontation of character, on a social level, and often over a trivial subject, is one of Jane Austen's most skilfully employed methods. Consider the following incident from *Sense and Sensibility*. The Palmers, together with Mrs Jennings and Lady Middleton, have called upon the Dashwoods: Mr. Palmer 'entered the room with a look of self-consequence, slightly bowed to the ladies, without speaking a word, and, after briefly surveying them and their apartments, took up a newspaper from the table and continued to read it as long as he staid' (*19*, 106). Mrs. Jennings leads the conversation among the ladies:

> '... I can't help wishing they had not travelled quite so fast ... for you know (nodding significantly and pointing to her daughter) it was wrong in her situation. I wanted her to stay at home and rest this morning, but she would come with us; she longed so much to see you all!'
>
> Mrs. Palmer laughed, and said it would not do her any harm.
>
> 'She [Mrs. Palmer] expects to be confined in February', continued Mrs. Jennings.
>
> Lady Middleton could no longer endure such a conversation, and therefore exerted herself to ask Mr. Palmer if there was any news in the paper.
>
> 'No, none at all', he replied, and read on.　　　*19*, 107-108

To take such an incident to pieces is like having to explain a joke, but some analysis shows us her method. Three characters have clashed and so revealed themselves. Mrs. Jennings' vulgarity in commenting upon Mrs. Palmer's pregnancy arouses the supine Lady Middleton to ask a typically inane question of her brother-in-law, and he, characteristically declining to have any truck with his in-laws, refuses to help her out by changing the topic of conversation. His comment, given his action, is of course ironic. (If there is no news in the paper, why does he go on reading?) It is also extremely rude.

The smallest civilities are observed by Jane Austen as a means of revealing character:

> 'Well, I believe, if you will excuse me, Mr. Knightley, if you will not consider me as doing a very rude thing, I shall take Emma's advice and go out for a quarter of an hour. As the sun is out, I believe I had better take my three turns while I can. I treat you without ceremony, Mr. Knightley. We invalids think we are privileged people.'
>
> 'My dear sir, do not make a stranger of me.'
>
> 'I leave an excellent substitute in my daughter. Emma will be happy to entertain you. And therefore I think I will beg your excuse and take my three turns—my winter walk.'
>
> 'You cannot do better, sir.'
>
> 'I would ask for the pleasure of your company, Mr. Knightley, but I am a very slow walker, and my pace would be tedious to you; and besides, you have another long walk before you, to Donwell Abbey.'
>
> 'Thank you, sir, thank you; I am going this moment myself; and I think the sooner *you* go the better. I will fetch your great-coat and open the garden door for you.' EMMA *8*, 57-58

Garrulity versus the man of few words and decisive action. Garrulity is, in *Emma*, the source of much comedy.

Reactions to trivial or unimportant objects are also revealing of character. Thus Harriet's criticism of Robert Martin's letter as being so short reveals her shallowness. The examination of the fans painted by Elinor evokes the venom of Mrs. Ferrars, her daughter's attempt at smoothing this over, and Marianne's passionate defence of her sister. Perhaps the best known example is the bother over Fanny Price's cross and chain in *Mansfield Park*, but in a few words a great deal can be done:

> 'If I were as rich as Mr. Darcy,' cried a young Lucas who came with his sisters, 'I should not care how proud I was. I would keep a pack of foxhounds, and drink a bottle of wine every day.'
>
> 'Then you would drink a great deal more than you ought,' said Mrs. Bennet; 'and if I were to see you at it I should take away your bottle directly.'

The boy protested that she should not; she continued to
declare that she would, and the argument ended only with the
visit.   PRIDE AND PREJUDICE 5, 20

The great deal that is being done in this passage is the revelation
of Mrs. Bennet's character. The author's direct comment early
in the novel: 'She was a woman of mean understanding, little
information, and uncertain temper' (*1*, 5) is being given body
in the passage above, for such is the intelligence and understanding of Mrs. Bennet that a whole visit will be frittered away
in a 'will/will not' argument with a *boy*.

The sterling worth of the heroine's character is often revealed
in relation to some simple incident or event. Anne Elliot alone
does not lose her head after Louisa Musgrove's fall on the Cobb
at Lyme. The nature of Elizabeth Bennet is shown on the first
visit to Rosings. She alone is unafraid:

> When they ascended the steps to the hall, Maria's alarm was
> every moment increasing, and even Sir William did not look
> perfectly calm.—Elizabeth's courage did not fail her. She had
> heard nothing of Lady Catherine that spoke her awful from any
> extraordinary talents or miraculous virtue, and the mere stateli-
> ness of money and rank, she thought she could witness without
> trepidation. . . .
>
> In spite of having been at St. James's, Sir William was so
> completely awed by the grandeur surrounding him, that he
> had but just courage enough to make a very low bow, and take
> his seat without saying a word; and his daughter, frightened
> almost out of her senses, sat on the edge of her chair, not
> knowing which way to look. Elizabeth found herself quite
> equal to the scene, and could observe the three ladies before her
> composedly.   PRIDE AND PREJUDICE 29, 161–162

REVELATION THROUGH DIALOGUE

Interplay of character in Jane Austen's novels generally takes
place through dialogue rather than through incident. In the case
of Fanny Price, who rarely has very much to say, this is not
quite so true, but in the case of the other heroines discussion is
very important. The opinion expressed by a character, or the

way in which he or she discusses a topic, is often a pointer as to their nature.

The dialogue between Elizabeth and Darcy not only reveals effectively the antagonism between the two of them, but also the intelligence of both.

'Sir William's interruption has made me forget what we were talking of.'

'I do not think we were speaking at all. Sir William could not have interrupted any two people in the room who had less to say for themselves.—We have tried two or three subjects already without success, and what we are to talk of next I cannot imagine.'

'What think you of books?' said he, smiling.

'Books—Oh! no.—I am sure we never read the same, or not with the same feelings.'

'I am sorry you think so; but if that be the case, there can at least be no want of subject.—We may compare our different opinions.'

'No—I cannot talk of books in a ball-room; my head is always full of something else.'

'The *present* always occupies you in such scenes—does it?' said he, with a look of doubt.

PRIDE AND PREJUDICE *18*, 93

Or, as in the case of Darcy's first proposal of marriage to Elizabeth, their forcefully expressed opinions provide us with ample indication of the strength of their personalities:

'But disguise of every sort is my abhorrence. Nor am I ashamed of the feelings I related. They were natural and just. Could you expect me to rejoice in the inferiority of your connections? To congratulate myself on the hope of relations, whose condition in life is so decidedly beneath my own?'

Elizabeth felt herself growing more angry every moment; yet she tried to the utmost to speak with composure when she said,

'You are mistaken, Mr. Darcy, if you suppose that the mode of your declaration affected me in any other way, than as it spared me the concern which I might have felt in refusing you, had you behaved in a more gentleman-like manner.'

She saw him start at this, but he said nothing, and she continued,

'You could not have made me the offer of your hand in any possible way that would have tempted me to accept it.'

Again his astonishment was obvious; and he looked at her with an expression of mingled incredulity and mortification. She went on.

'From the very beginning, from the first moment I may almost say, of my acquaintance with you, your manners impressing me with the fullest belief of your arrogance, your conceit, and your selfish disdain of the feelings of others, were such as to form that ground-work of disapprobation, on which succeeding events have built so immoveable a dislike. . . .'

34, 192-193

But dialogue does not always reveal characters so straightforwardly. Language can be used as a disguise by a character. It may be an attractive veil for an unsound nature.

Let us consider two arguments, one from Elizabeth Bennet, the other from Mary Crawford. Both are lively, witty females, yet one is a heroine, the other is rejected. Why is this? Where does the difference lie?

In *Pride and Prejudice*, Elizabeth, staying at Netherfield, joins in the conversation in the drawing-room, which turns on the nature of female accomplishments. Miss Bingley draws up a long list of requirements for a woman to be considered accomplished, and Darcy adds:

'All this she must possess . . . and to all this she must yet add something more substantial, in the improvement of her mind by extensive reading.'

'I am no longer surprised at your knowing *only* six accomplished women. I rather wonder now at your knowing *any*' [says Elizabeth].

'Are you so severe upon your own sex, as to doubt the possibility of all this?'

'*I* never saw such a woman. *I* never saw such capacity, and taste, and application, and elegance, as you describe, united.'

8, 39-40

Elizabeth is speaking personally, but we accept her answer as honest, and we feel that she is right. Miss Bingley's list was a deliberate affectation and carried with it the suggestion that she was describing her own view of herself. Elizabeth, in disclaiming it, is appealing to common sense and reason, even though she is giving a personal opinion.

In *Mansfield Park*, in the wood at Sotherton, Mary and Edmund begin an argument on the distance they have walked. Mary insists it must be a mile, though Edmund denies it with appeals to reason—the view through the wood, and the time they have been walking:

> 'But if you remember, before we left the first great path, we saw directly to the end of it. We looked down the whole vista, and saw it closed by iron gates, and it could not have been more than a furlong in length.'
>
> 'Oh! I know nothing of your furlongs, but I am sure it is a very long wood; and that we have been winding in and out ever since we came into it; and therefore when I say that we have walked a mile in it, I must speak within compass.'
>
> 'We have been exactly a quarter of an hour here,' said Edmund, taking out his watch. 'Do you think we are walking four miles an hour?'
>
> 'Oh! do not attack me with your watch. A watch is always too fast or too slow. I cannot be dictated to by a watch.' *9, 95*

Mary is being witty, and deliberately outrageous, but in her refusal to see reason, her insistence on her personal impressions, and her sliding away from the main point there is the suggestion of superficiality and frivolity, self-interest and a lack of concern for the truth of an argument, which does not appear in Elizabeth's retorts.

There is something of this in Emma also, and *her* vanity and blindness to the truth result in a series of misadventures. In *Mansfield Park*, the level is serious; in *Emma* it is comic:

> 'And you have forgotten one matter of joy to me', said Emma, 'and a very considerable one—that I made the match myself. I made the match, you know, four years ago . . . and when such

success has blessed me in this instance, dear papa, you cannot think that I shall leave off match-making.'

'I do not understand what you mean by "success"', said Mr. Knightley. 'Success supposes endeavour. Your time has been properly and delicately spent, if you have been endeavouring for the last four years to bring about this marriage. . . . why do you talk of success? where is your merit?—what are you proud of?—you made a lucky guess; and *that* is all that can be said.'

'And have you never known the pleasure and triumph of a lucky guess?—I pity you . . . for depend upon it, a lucky guess is never merely luck. . . .'   *1*, 11-13

Emma is deliberately prevaricating here and deliberately ignoring the seriousness of Mr. Knightley's condemnation of 'match-making' as an improper and indelicate occupation. Instead she takes up only his suggestion of her 'lucky guess' and claims that as 'never merely luck' in order to avoid his more serious criticism.

In *Sense and Sensibility*, Willoughby makes use of the same, personal and frivolous arguments, putting reason out of sight, and this is a suspicious aspect of his character:

'Miss Dashwood', cried Willoughby, 'you are now using me unkindly. You are endeavouring to disarm me by reason, and to convince me against my will. But it will not do. You shall find me as stubborn as you can be artful. I have three unanswerable reasons for disliking Colonel Brandon: he has threatened me with rain when I wanted it to be fine; he has found fault with the hanging of my curricle, and I cannot persuade him to buy my brown mare. If it will be any satisfaction to you, however, to be told, that I believe his character to be in other respects irreproachable, I am ready to confess it. And in return for an acknowledgement, which must give me some pain, you cannot deny me the privilege of disliking him as much as ever.'

10, 51-52

The reader may well be disarmed by such arguments, but in Jane Austen's world, if he is, he will be missing a definite clue as to character which she is putting in the reader's way, as well as in the way of the other characters in the novel.

126

ther methods of character delineation are really an extension
f the character sketch. In all the novels there is a great deal of
ossip. Everybody is interested in everybody else, and characters
e discussed at length and opinions passed on them, though,
enerally speaking, the valuable opinions are in the hands of
nly a few, more intelligent characters, and rightness of judge-
ient will belong eventually only to them.

The beginning of *Pride and Prejudice* is all gossip, gossip
eated ironically, showing how rumour distorts truth—a fact
lizabeth might have kept in mind where Darcy was concerned.
ingley is introduced through Mrs. Long's report to Mrs.
ennet about his arrival; later Lady Lucas started the idea of his
eing gone to London only to get a large party for the ball; and
report soon followed that Mr. Bingley was to bring 'twelve
dies and seven gentlemen' as his guests. At the Assembly, a
eport . . . was in general circulation within five minutes after
Darcy's] entrance, of his having ten thousand a year' (*3*, 10).
ydia and Catherine find their visits to their aunt 'productive
f the most interesting intelligence. Every day added something
) their knowledge of the officers' names and connections . . .'
7, 28), though they are not so well informed as to know that the
entlemen from Netherfield are to dine with the officers. Lady
Catherine de Bourgh is brought to Longbourn by a 'report of
most alarming nature' regarding Elizabeth and Darcy.

In *Emma*, Mr. Knightley, coming to tell Emma the news of
Ir. Elton's engagement, is forestalled by Miss Bates who only
ve minutes earlier had heard the news from Mrs. Cole who had
nly just got it from her husband.

'Human nature', writes Jane Austen, 'is so well disposed
owards those who are in interesting situations, that a young
erson, who either marries or dies, is sure of being kindly spoken
f' (*E. 22*, 181). In other situations, we know from her novels
hat they are likely to be ill-spoken of. In the case of Jane
'airfax—who refuses to gossip—there is, ironically, no report
hat Emma can catch hold of, and she is forced to invent scandal
bout Jane for herself.

The reader is led, between the character-sketches, the charac ters themselves speaking and acting, and the opinions of other about them, to reason and wonder and draw his own con clusions. Where the simpler characters are concerned, there is n difficulty—one has no doubts about a Mrs. Allen or a Mr Woodhouse. But one has doubts about major characters.

At the Longbourn Assembly, Mr. Darcy is found to be proud

> Mr. Darcy danced only once with Mrs. Hurst and once with Miss Bingley, declined being introduced to any other lady, an spent the rest of the evening in walking about the room, speaking occasionally to one of his own party. PRIDE AND PREJUDICE 3, 1

He refuses to dance with Elizabeth—'I am in no humour a present to give consequence to young ladies who are slighted by other men' (3, 12). Wickham's report of Darcy's character damns him completely—as he intends it should, and it late results in Elizabeth refusing his offer of marriage. Darcy's letter to her afterwards clears his character in part, and the opinions of his housekeeper at Pemberley provide another aspect of his character—he is good-natured, 'the best landlord, and the best master ... that ever lived' (43, 249). After this, it only requires his own behaviour at Pemberley to reveal his different nature Elizabeth, though she does not realise it, is partly in the grip o opinion and gossip where Darcy is concerned.

Frank Churchill's character is never entirely steady in the hands of the Highbury gossips. And Chapter 5 of *Emma* is wholly taken up by a discussion of the heroine's character by Knightley and Mrs. Weston. Mrs. Weston presents the favourable view, Mr. Knightley the unfavourable, and by the end of the chapter we are pretty well in possession of complete knowledge of Emma's nature and the faults likely to get her into trouble. 'She will never submit to any thing requiring industry and patience, and a subjection of the fancy to the understanding' (5, 37). We learn of her cleverness, and her self-will, that she is full of health and beauty. As Mr. Knightley points out, she is not vain—'her vanity lies another way' (5, 39). Yet she is a good daughter, a kind sister, and a true friend.

In the same way, Edmund and Fanny discuss Mary Crawford n Chapter 7 of *Mansfield Park*. Mary is praised for her appearance, but criticised on the ground that she discussed her uncle ndecorously. She is granted 'a lively mind', without ill-humour —'perfectly feminine' (*7, 64*).

In *Persuasion*, Anne Elliot is shown to be at one time caught between the cross-tides of gossip, and her method of extricating herself reveals something of her character:

> One of the least agreeable circumstances of her residence there, was her being treated with too much confidence by all parties, and being too much in the secret of the complaints of each house.   *6, 44*

> How was Anne to set all these matters to rights? She could do little more than listen patiently, soften every grievance, and excuse each to the other; give them all hints of the forbearance necessary between such near neighbours, and make those hints broadest which were meant for her sister's benefit.   *6, 46*

The Crofts' opinion of the Musgrove sisters makes us suspect that Captain Wentworth, in spite of appearances, will not marry either:

> 'And very nice young ladies they both are; I hardly know one from the other.'
> 'Very good humoured, unaffected girls, indeed,' said Mrs. Croft, in a tone of calmer praise, such as made Anne suspect that her keener powers might not consider either of them as quite worthy of her brother. . .   PERSUASION *10, 92*

Sir Walter Elliot, we are told, is a vain man, but this is brought home to us indirectly and ironically through another character. Admiral Croft, speaking of the alterations he has made since becoming tenant of Kellynch Hall, remarks to Anne:

> 'I have done very little besides sending away some of the large looking-glasses from my dressing-room, which was your father's. A very good man, and very much the gentleman I am sure—but I should think, Miss Elliot,' (looking with serious reflection) 'I should think he must be rather a dressy man for

his time of life.—Such a number of looking-glasses! oh, Lord! there was no getting away from oneself [a telling comment on both characters]. So I got Sophy to lend me a hand, and we soon shifted their quarters; and now I am quite snug, with my little shaving glass in one corner, and another great thing that I never go near.'   PERSUASION *13*, 127-128

A vivid commentary, through physical objects, on Sir Walter's vanity and the Admiral's lack of it.

Mrs. Elton, in *Emma*, by first report was 'discovered to have every recommendation of person and mind; to be handsome, elegant, highly accomplished, and perfectly amiable' (*22*, 181). Emma is not taken in by this, though her reasons for disbelieving it might not be grounded on anything very objective. Harriet *is* taken in, inevitably, by public opinion, and her first view of Mrs. Elton convinces her that she is 'beautiful', 'very charming'. But Emma, after a first meeting, decides that she is 'a vain woman, extremely well satisfied with herself, and thinking much of her own importance' (*32*, 272), an opinion which is borne out by the novel. The rest of Highbury, however, 'disposed to commend, or not in the habit of judging', 'were very well satisfied', and Mr. Weston remarks that she 'is a good-natured woman after all.'

Anne Elliot gains a great deal of the reader's sympathy from being forced to hear, at second-hand, Captain Wentworth's opinion of her:

> 'Captain Wentworth is not very gallant by you, Anne, though he was so attentive to me. Henrietta asked him what he thought of you, when they went away; and he said, "You were so altered he should not have known you again." '
>
> PERSUASION *7*, 60

We sympathise at this hurt, especially since Anne, lacking confidence, acknowledges it as true, yet can also admit that the years have only improved him.

It is, then, from a number of different reports that the heroines are left to make up their minds about the people around them, and they form their opinions according to their natures.

Marianne, Emma, and Elizabeth are hasty, a girl like Elinor judges objectively, and Fanny Price always comes to the right conclusion.

CHARACTER IN PLOT

In her later novels Jane Austen is more skilful in integrating her minor characters into the plot. Let us consider this development by examining two characters—Mrs. Bennet in *Pride and Prejudice* and Miss Bates in *Emma*. Both are garrulous women of few ideas. Mrs. Bennet is concerned to get her daughters married, to fulminate against the entail, and to take an interest in the superficialities of life. Her reaction to her daughter's elopement is typical:

> 'Oh! my dear brother', replied Mrs. Bennet, 'that is exactly what I could most wish for. And now do, when you get to town, find them out, wherever they may be; and if they are not married already, *make* them marry. And as for wedding clothes, do not let them wait for that, but tell Lydia she shall have as much money as she chuses, to buy them, after they are married. And, above all things, keep Mr. Bennet from fighting. Tell him what a dreadful state I am in,—that I am frightened out of my wits; and have such tremblings, such flutterings, all over me, such spasms in my side, and pains in my head, and such beatings at heart, that I can get no rest by night nor by day. And tell my dear Lydia, not to give any directions about her clothes, till she has seen me, for she does not know which are the best warehouses.'

PRIDE AND PREJUDICE *47*, 288

Her concern with the wedding clothes, with her own nerves and sufferings, and her inability to take in the true nature of the situation—these are the responses we would expect from Mrs. Bennet.

Miss Bates is regarded as a terrible bore, especially by Emma, but her meanderings are generally more to the point of the plot than are Mrs. Bennet's. A great deal of the idea of Highbury as a community—and it is a most convincing community—comes from Miss Bates:

'For, would you believe it, Miss Woodhouse, there he is, in the most obliging manner in the world, fastening in the rivet of my mother's spectacles.—The rivet came out, you know, this morning.—So very obliging!—For my mother had no use of her spectacles—could not put them on. And, by the bye, every body ought to have two pair of spectacles; they should indeed. Jane said so. I meant to take them over to John Saunders the first thing I did, but something or other hindered me all the morning; first one thing, then another, there is no saying what, you know. At one time Patty came to say she thought the kitchen chimney wanted sweeping. Oh! said I, Patty do not come with your bad news to me. Here is the rivet of your mistress's spectacles out. Then the baked apples came home, Mrs. Wallis sent them by her boy; they are extremely civil and obliging to us, the Wallises, always—I have heard some people say that Mrs. Wallis can be uncivil and give a very rude answer, but we have never known any thing but the greatest attention from them. And it cannot be for the value of our custom now, for what is our consumption of bread, you know? Only three of us—besides dear Jane at present—and she really eats nothing —makes such a shocking breakfast, you would be quite fright- ened if you saw it. I dare not let my mother know how little she eats—so I say one thing and then I say another, and it passes off. But about the middle of the day she gets hungry, and there is nothing she likes so well as these baked apples, and they are extremely wholesome. . . .' EMMA 27, 236-237

It is little wonder that, after an interruption, Emma 'wondered on what, of all the medley, she would fix' to go on talking about as her main theme.

The inconsequence and muddle here are based on the same principle as that lying behind Mrs. Bennet's speech—the selection of topic depending upon the process of thought association within the speaker's mind. Of course, such a con- fusion, such an inability to deal with subjects in an orderly fashion, indicates the stupidity and confusion of the speaker, but we feel a much greater sympathy for Miss Bates than for Mrs. Bennet. Miss Bates is not selfish—her confusion derives in part from her kind-heartedness, her concern for everyone, and desire to do everyone justice, and especially her concern for Jane Fairfax.

The confusion in Miss Bates' speech represents a greater degree of ability on Jane Austen's part. The sentence becomes broken and confused as does the thought process, yet Miss Bates, and Jane Austen, eventually find their way through the confusion. And from Miss Bates we learn, incidentally, of Patty their maid, John Saunders the village silversmith, Mrs. Wallis the baker's wife; of broken spectacles, baked apples, the kitchen chimney and the bread bill of the Bates family—such trivia of the daily events of village life in Highbury which contrive to fill up Miss Bates' morning in such a hectic fashion. And, of course, the irony is that it is not all trivia—the state of Jane Fairfax's health, Frank Churchill's unaccountable kindness to her grandmother, are important to the plot, since through them we are being led to an understanding of the relationship between Jane and Frank, and made to understand Emma's ignorance of it. What the reader eventually pieces together out of the confusion of Miss Bates' thoughts, Emma misses because she is only bored by the confusion.

HUMAN NATURE—REPETITION AND VARIETY

Certain types of character appear several times in Jane Austen's novels, though perhaps it would be more accurate to say that she treats repetitively certain human traits. Flattery and vanity are related characteristics and are frequently treated together.

The toady, the person who ingratiates himself with others for various reasons, is a recurrent character in her novels. The presence of a toady implies, of course, flattery and deception on his part, and an acute understanding of the person he is flattering. It also brings out the weakness of the person being flattered. Thus, Mr. Collins panders to Lady Catherine's snobbishness and self-importance though he is so obvious and naïve in his efforts that we cannot but laugh at him:

'. . . it is happy for you [says Mr. Bennet] that you possess the talent of flattering with delicacy. May I ask whether these pleasing attentions proceed from the impulse of the moment, or are the result of previous study?'

'They arise chiefly from what is passing at the time, and though I sometimes amuse myself with suggesting and arranging such little elegant compliments as may be adapted to ordinary occasions, I always wish to give them as unstudied an air as possible.' PRIDE AND PREJUDICE *14*, 68

Other flatterers are less comic, but equally perceptively drawn. Miss Bingley flatters Darcy in her attempts to win him, but Darcy's character is proof against such arts:

'How delighted Miss Darcy will be to receive such a letter!' He made no answer.
'You write uncommonly fast.'
'You are mistaken. I write rather slowly.'
'How many letters you must have occasion to write in the course of the year! Letters of business too! How odious I should think them!'
'It is fortunate, then, that they fall to my lot instead of to yours.'
'Pray tell your sister that I long to see her.'
'I have already told her so once, by your desire.'
'I am afraid you do not like your pen. Let me mend it for you. I mend pens remarkably well.'
'Thank you—but I always mend my own.'
'How can you contrive to write so even?'
He was silent. PRIDE AND PREJUDICE *10*, 47-48

The Misses Steele in *Sense and Sensibility*, dealing only with Lady Middleton's pride in her children, have more success:

With her children they were in continual raptures, extolling their beauty, courting their notice, and humouring all their whims; and such of their time as could be spared from the importunate demands which this politeness made on it, was spent in admiration of whatever her ladyship was doing, if she happened to be doing any thing, or in taking patterns of some elegant new dress, in which her appearance the day before had thrown them into unceasing delight. Fortunately for those who pay their court through such foibles, a fond mother, though, in pursuit of praise for her children, the most rapacious of human beings, is likewise the most credulous; her demands are exorbitant; but she will swallow any thing. . . .   *21*, 120

Mrs. Norris is the most persistent and most rasping of the flatterers, and it is a measure of Sir Thomas Bertram's vanity and lack of perception that he is taken in by her:

'My dear Sir Thomas, I perfectly comprehend you, and do justice to the generosity and delicacy of your notions, which indeed are quite of a piece with your general conduct. . . .'

MANSFIELD PARK *1*, 6

It is less surprising, therefore, that Sir Walter Elliot and Elizabeth, with all the Elliot pride and none of Sir Thomas' sternness of principle, should fall victims to the insinuations of Mrs. Clay:

'Quite delightful!' cried Mrs. Clay, not daring, however, to turn her eyes towards Anne. 'Exactly like father and son! Dear Miss Elliot, may I not say father and son?'   PERSUASION, *22*, 213

Mrs. Clay, playing for high stakes, is fully aware of what she is about, and fully aware that other people, if not the Elliots, might see through her.

The strangest aspect of this theme of the flatterer occurs in *Emma*, where Emma herself is at the mercy of flatterers, some with an intention to deceive her, others with only affection as their motive. Her father is one of the worst offenders: 'Ah! my dear, I wish you would not make matches and foretel things, for whatever you say always comes to pass' (*1*, 12); 'Emma never thinks of herself, if she can do good to others' (*1*, 13); 'But you will do every thing right. I need not tell you what is to be done' (*25*, 210). Harriet is equally naïve in her praise and admiration; 'Whatever you say is always right' (*25*, 74); 'I do so wonder, Miss Woodhouse, that you should not be married . . . so charming as you are!' (*10*, 84).

Mr. Elton, at least while he has marriage to her in view, is a most conscious flatterer: 'You have given Miss Smith all that she required . . . you have made her graceful and easy . . . the attractions you have added are infinitely superior to what she received from nature' (*6*, 42); 'I know what your drawings are.

How could you suppose me ignorant? Is not this room rich in specimens of your landscapes and flowers . . .?' (6, 43). It is Emma's merit that she disregards most of the flattery she encounters. True, she is conceited enough not to require its support, but she is also capable of seeing through the excesses of Mr. Elton's compliments: 'Yes, good man!—thought Emma —but what has all that to do with taking likenesses? You know nothing of drawing. Don't pretend to be in raptures about mine. Keep your raptures for Harriet's face' (6, 43).

Frank Churchill's flattery is equally conscious, more contrived, and ironical. Discussing the water-party at which Jane Fairfax and the Dixons were present, Emma says:

> 'If I had been there, I think I should have made some discoveries.'
> 'I dare say you would; but I, simple I, saw nothing but the fact, that Miss Fairfax was nearly dashed from the vessel and that Mr. Dixon caught her.—It was the work of a moment. And though the consequent shock and alarm was very great and much more durable . . . yet that was too general a sensation for any thing of peculiar anxiety to be observable. I do not mean to say, however, that you might not have made discoveries.'
>
> 26, 218

Selfish insipidity is another recurring trait in the novels. Lady Middleton, Mrs. John Dashwood, Mrs. Allen, Lady Bertram are all characterized by this; but Lady Middleton concentrates on elegance and her children, Mrs. Dashwood on her money, Mrs. Allen on dress, and Lady Bertram on her 'pug'. And each has her individual way of expressing herself. The selfish, vain man who is inordinately fond of his food and very fussy about it appears in Mr. Palmer, Dr. Grant, Mr. Woodhouse and General Tilney.

This is a further aspect of Jane Austen's variety in a narrow compass which affects her range of characters. The limitations in which she worked imposed upon her repetitions of theme, situations, and human traits, but she was able to bring to each one, each time, a new and original treatment.

9

The Physical and Social Background

THE SOCIAL BACKGROUND

We have already referred to the impórtance of gossip in the novels as a means of characterization—either by enlightening us as to a person's character or by confusing the issue. This background of gossip and rumour has more to do in the novels. It is responsible to some extent for giving the impression of a solid social background, a convincing society behind the characters. And since it implies, and arises from, constant and close social contacts within a society, it is connected with the workings of the plot. In addition, it is responsible for that impression of constant surveillance, of lack of privacy in small societies. This is linked with the need her heroines in particular feel, and which Jane Austen advocates, for restraint in the expressing and revealing of one's emotions, the need for control and propriety.

The pressures of society in this form vary in importance in the novels. In *Northanger Abbey*, for example, there is really only John Thorpe who is a gossip and who spreads a false rumour as to Catherine's being an heiress, which causes General Tilney to look on her favourably as a wife for his son. Apart from that, there is Henry Tilney's forceful and telling comment on the England of that day when he is disabusing Catherine of her Gothic misconceptions:

> Does our education prepare us for such atrocities? Do our laws connive at them? Could they be perpetrated without being known, in a country like this, where social and literary inter-course is on such a footing; *where every man is surrounded by a*

> neighbourhood of voluntary spies* and where roads and news-
> papers lay every thing open? (my italics)   24, 197-198

(*For 'voluntary spies' we should, of course, read 'local gossips'.)

When they move to Barton, the Dashwoods find themselves almost forcibly drawn into intimate relationship with the Middleton household—a fact which Marianne objects to strongly: 'The rent of this cottage is said to be low; but we have it on very hard terms, if we are to dine at the park whenever any one is staying either with them, or with us' (*S. & S. 19*, 109). Mrs. Jennings is constantly speculating on the girls' lovers, and is most rude in attempting to find out what business takes Colonel Brandon away so suddenly. The pressure of the requirements of society is constantly felt when Marianne is so distressed by Willoughby's behaviour in the presence of visitors and guests at Mrs. Jennings' house and table. Marianne, however unjustly, is forced into saying: 'All that she [Mrs. Jennings] wants is gossip, and she only likes me now because I supply it' (*S. & S. 31*, 201). Mrs. Palmer's sympathy is shown:

> in procuring all the particulars in her power of the approaching marriage, and communicating them to Elinor. She could soon tell at what coachmaker's the new carriage was building, by what painter Mr. Willoughby's portrait was drawn, and at what warehouse Miss Grey's clothes might be seen.   32, 215

In *Mansfield Park*, there is such a sense of isolation about the Park itself, that rumour and gossip are at a minimum—indeed there is no sense of a social community in the novel, except perhaps at Portsmouth. Social intercourse is limited strictly to the Park and the vicarage. But the strong social pressures exist at Uppercross in *Persuasion:*

> The two families were so continually meeting, so much in the habit of running in and out of each other's house at all hours. . . .
> 5, 36

> Anne . . . admired again the sort of necessity which the family habits seemed to produce, of every thing being to be communicated, and every thing being to be done together, however undesired and inconvenient.   10, 83

138

In *Emma* this background of rumour and gossip is very strong. 'There was a strange rumour in Highbury of all the little Perrys being seen with a slice of Mrs. Weston's wedding-cake in their hands; but Mr. Woodhouse would never believe it' (*2, 19*). And 'Emma afterwards heard that Jane Fairfax had been seen wandering about the meadows, at some distance from Highbury, on the afternoon of the very day on which she had, under the plea of being unequal to any exercise, so peremptorily refused to go out with her in the carriage' (*45, 391*).

Miss Bates's meanderings, while they are a significant comic aspect of the novel, make us constantly aware of the often embarrassingly close proximity of Highbury lives, of the spread of gossip, and the fear of giving offence:

> 'Indeed they are very delightful apples, and Mrs. Wallis does them full justice—only we do not have them baked more than twice, and Mr. Woodhouse made us promise to have them done three times—but Miss Woodhouse will be so good as not to mention it.' EMMA, *27, 238*

> 'I would not have Mr. Knightley know any thing about it for the world! He would be so very . . . I wanted to keep it from Jane's knowledge; but unluckily, I had mentioned it before I was aware.' *27, 239*

> 'Grandmamma was quite well, had a charming evening with Mr· Woodhouse, a vast deal of chat, and backgammon. . . . I was telling you of your grandmamma, Jane,—There was a little disappointment . . . there was a delicate fricassee of sweetbread and some asparagus brought in at first, and good Mr. Wood-house, not thinking the asparagus quite boiled enough, sent it all out again. Now there is nothing grandmamma loves better than sweetbread and asparagus—so she was rather disappointed, but we agreed we would not speak of it to any body, for fear of its getting round to dear Miss Woodhouse. . . .' *38, 329-330*

THE PHYSICAL BACKGROUND

1. Descriptions of Place

Few writers have been so sparing in their descriptions of the physical settings of their novels. Jane Austen can do a great deal with half a sentence towards giving the reader a sufficient idea of the background to a scene. In *Persuasion*, Anne finds Mary lying 'on the faded sofa of the pretty little drawing-room, the once elegant furniture of which had been gradually growing shabby, under the influence of four summers and two children. . . .' (*5*, 37). The impression of the assembly at Bath is given through Catherine Morland's progress through the ballroom: '. . . the room [was] crowded, and the two ladies squeezed in as well as they could . . . . to proceed along the room was by no means the way to disengage themselves from the crowd; it seemed rather to increase as they went on . . . . by a continued exertion of strength and ingenuity they found themselves at last in the passage behind the highest bench' (*N. A. 2,* 20-21). And just as briefly, she can give an impression of the weather so as to convey to our senses what must be felt by her characters: 'A cold stormy rain set in, and nothing of July appeared but in the trees and shrubs, which the wind was despoiling, and the length of the day, which only made such cruel sights the longer visible' (*E. 48,* 421). When Anne leaves Uppercross, there is 'a small thick rain almost blotting out the very few objects ever to be discerned from the windows . . . the cottage, with its black, dripping, and comfortless veranda . . .' (*P. 13,* 123).

Yet her descriptions of setting are of the eighteenth century in that they are rarely particularised. We see this in her descriptions of great houses, such as Pemberley and Donwell Abbey:

> They gradually ascended for half a mile, and then found themselves at the top of a considerable eminence, where the wood ceased, and the eye was instantly caught by Pemberley House, situated on the opposite side of a valley, into which the road with some abruptness wound. It was a large, handsome, stone building, standing well on rising ground, and backed by a ridge of high woody hills;—and in front, a stream of some natural importance was swelled into greater, but without any artificial appearance. PRIDE AND PREJUDICE *43,* 245

Nothing here is calculated to inspire strong emotional response

140

in the reader—only approval of something in generally good, not extravagant, taste. Nothing is extraordinary, exaggerated or made personal or particular. The hill is only 'a considerable eminence'. Pemberley House is a 'large, handsome, stone building'. Standing on 'rising ground' it has 'high woody hills' behind and a stream in front. There has been some attempt at landscape gardening—the stream has been enlarged, but not noticeably so. These are the 'prominent and striking features, as recall the original to the mind' which Dr. Johnson approved of in descriptions.

Compare this with Charlotte Brontë's description of Mr. Rochester's house, Thornfield. Jane Eyre, descending into the hall looked:

> ... at some pictures on the walls ... at a bronze lamp pendant from the ceiling, at a great clock whose case was of oak curiously carved, and ebon black with time and rubbing. ... It was a fine autumn morning. ... I looked up and surveyed the front of the mansion. It was three stories high, of proportions not vast, though considerable; a gentleman's manor-house, not a noble-man's seat: battlements round the top gave it a picturesque look. Its gray front stood out well from the background of a rookery, whose cawing tenants were now on the wing. They flew over the lawn and grounds to alight in a great meadow, from which these were separated by a sunk fence, and where an array of mighty old thorn trees, strong, knotty, and broad as oaks, at once explained the etymology of the mansion's designation. Farther off were hills ... quiet and lonely hills enough and seeming to embrace Thornfield with a seclusion. ...
>
> JANE EYRE, Chap. II

One notices the details that a writer like Charlotte Brontë found it necessary to give—the carved clock, the number of storeys, the battlements, rookery, etc. Not only this, but there are emotional connections associated with the details—time and rubbing have made the clock case black, the house is picturesque, the thorn trees strong and knotty, the hills 'embrace' the house.

I do not wish to suggest that one method of description is superior to the other. What I would point out is that Jane

Austen's intention and interest is centred on her characters. Their surroundings are merely sketched in.

2. *The Importance of Setting*

Yet for a writer who does not dwell on long, detailed, and emotive descriptions of place, setting can be extremely important in her work. The atmosphere and feeling of the individual novels is to some extent determined by the nature of the individual setting.

Sense and Sensibility and *Pride and Prejudice* are novels in which setting is at a minimum—it is left mainly to the imagination of the reader to fit in the details of background against which the active and full social life of the characters is played out. In *Sense and Sensibility*, as so often in her novels, we are aware of scenery mainly through the eyes of characters—in this case the connection is with the theme of sensibility:

> 'Now, Edward', said [Marianne], calling his attention to the prospect, 'here is Barton valley. Look up it, and be tranquil if you can. Look at those hills! Did you ever see their equals? To the left is Barton park, amongst those woods and plantations . . . . And there, beneath that farthest hill, which rises with such grandeur, is our cottage.'
>
> 'It is a beautiful country,' he replied; 'but these bottoms must be dirty in winter.'
>
> *16*, 88

But there is little distinction in this novel among, for example, the Middletons' country home, Mrs. Jennings' town house, and Mrs. Palmer's home. Each takes its importance from the incidents that happen there—Willoughby and Marianne's intimacy at the first, Marianne's grief at the second, and her illness and near death at the third.

Similarly, in *Pride and Prejudice*, the emphasis is upon the actions, feelings, and conversations of the characters. Rosings is etched in more fully to give us the impression of wealth and pride, and Pemberley is described more extensively, but the rest is left to the reader.

a. Setting and Morality in 'Mansfield Park'

The setting of *Mansfield Park* emphasises the sombre morality of the theme. We have Fanny's 'White attic' and her 'East room', both cold, fireless, but offering privacy, and the abode of virtue. Indeed, the description of the old schoolroom, which Fanny makes her sitting-room, is remarkably detailed, and the room takes on a symbolic value reflecting the virtues of Fanny's nature:

> Her plants, her books—of which she had been a collector, from the first hour of her commanding a shilling [qualities of education and mind]—her writing desk, and her works of charity and ingenuity, were all within her reach . . . she could scarcely see an object in that room which had not an interesting remembrance connected with it . . . though she had known the pains of tyranny, of ridicule, and neglect [Christian suffering] . . . the whole was now so blended together, so harmonized by distance, that every former affliction had its charm [Christian forgiveness] . . .
>
> *16, 151-152*

The old, worn furniture satisfies Fanny's spirit of simplicity, and her love for her brother is represented by 'a small sketch of a ship . . . with H.M.S. *Antwerp* at the bottom.'

On the other hand, we have the disturbing of Sir Thomas' house, and his study, to make way for the theatricals. A sense of desecration comes from the presence of carpenters and scene-painters, the moving of book-cases, etc: '. . . I think a theatre ought not to be attempted.—[says Edmund] It would be taking liberties with my father's house in his absence which could not be justified . . .' And Tom retorts, 'His house shall not be hurt' (*M. P. 13*, 127). At Mansfield, there is no relief from the sense of solemn fitness, of correctness, and chill which comes from the setting, just as at Portsmouth there is no relief from the noise and disorder—a further tribulation to be borne silently and without complaint by Fanny, and from which she characteristically retires to the small bedroom she shares with Susan. And there the two girls virtuously and rewardingly employ themselves in reading and talking.

143

The natural setting in the novel seems to have no beauty of its own—for generally it only serves to emphasise Fanny's lack of vitality and to provide inconvenience for her in some way. If she is prevented from riding she soon grows pale, if she is out in the sun she gets a headache, the environment of Portsmouth affects her health and spirits. Even the visit to Sotherton proves too much for her health and strength: 'Every sort of exercise fatigues her so soon', as Edmund says. Fanny replies: 'I shall soon be rested . . . to sit in the shade on a fine day, and look upon verdure, is the most perfect refreshment' (9, 96).

The natural background at Sotherton becomes simply an excuse for intrigue and flirtation, forerunner of the final catastrophe in the novel, with Fanny as the watcher and judger. The iron gate into the park is locked, Mr. Rushworth is sent to get the key, leaving Maria and Henry Crawford together: '. . . that iron gate, that ha-ha, give me a feeling of restraint and hardship. I cannot get out, as the starling said', is Maria's comment, and with Crawford's help, she squeezes round the gate and disappears with him (10, 99). This is symbolic of her later desertion of her husband for Crawford. Mr. Rushworth and Julia, each arriving at different times, are each put out by this action. Even Mrs. Norris' love of getting something for nothing makes its impression on the natural background by obtruding itself upon the products of the estate:

> . . . she had found a morning of complete enjoyment—for the housekeeper . . . had taken her to the dairy, told her all about their cows, and given her the receipt for a famous cream cheese; and . . . the gardener . . . had shewn her all his choicest nursery of plants, and actually presented her with a very curious specimen of heath . . . . and Mrs. Norris, having fidgetted about, and obtained a few pheasants' eggs and a cream cheese from the housekeeper . . . was ready to lead the way.   10, 104-105

b. Background and Bounteousness in 'Emma'

In *Emma*, the natural background, while it changes with the four seasons of the year through which the novel turns, is never harsh, and the two houses of Donwell and Hartfield are bound up with this background. There is a sense of the bounteousness of nature provided by the frequent references to food. Donwell's apples and strawberries are of the finest kind; Hartfield pork is 'very small and delicate', and Miss Bates has her gift of pork salted and roasted—Mrs. Bates was afraid there was not 'a salting-pan large enough' and there is nothing she loves better than roast pork; at Christmas there is 'Mr. Weston's good wine', and John Knightley's little boys hurry back to Hartfield after a walk to 'ensure a quick despatch of the roast mutton and rice pudding'. Emma is constantly organizing evening meals for the old ladies who come to sit with her father and attempting to make sure they eat them:

> . . . with the real good-will of a mind delighted with its own ideas, did she then do all the honours of the meal, and help and recommend the minced chicken and scalloped oysters. . . .
> '. . . Miss Bates, let Emma help you to a *little* bit of tart—a *very* little bit. Ours are all apple tarts. You need not be afraid of unwholesome preserves here. I do not advise the custard.'
>
> EMMA *3*, 24-25

And Emma helps Mrs. Goddard and Mrs. Bates to 'large slices of cake and full glasses of wine'. At Miss Bates' there is sweet cake and baked apples. Gifts are always being sent—broth to the poor, arrowroot to Jane Fairfax, a pianoforte—dinners and cold collations always being prepared.

Comfort and wealth are part of the background, and although the novel is set in Surrey, it reminds us of Jane Austen's comment in a letter: 'Kent is the only place for happiness, Everybody is rich there.' Donwell is viewed by Emma with pride and complacency: '. . . low and sheltered—its ample gardens stretching down to meadows washed by a stream, of which the Abbey . . . had scarcely a sight—and its abundance of timber in rows and avenues. . . . The house was larger than Hartfield . . . . the residence of a family of such true gentility' (*E. 42*, 358). There is a 'broad short avenue of limes . . . . a charming walk' and a view of Abbey Mill Farm 'with meadows in front, and the river making a close and handsome curve around it. It was a sweet view—sweet to the eye and the mind. English verdure, English culture, English comfort, seen under a sun bright, without being oppressive' (*42*, 360). There is 'prosperity and beauty . . . rich pastures, spreading flocks, orchard in blossom, and light column of smoke ascending.'

Emma is set in a sunny, pleasant land. Even the poor Bateses are surrounded by generous neighbours by whose charity Miss Bates is constantly amazed—and indeed, Miss Bates is strongly connected with the theme of gratitude and satisfaction. Even the climate is rarely harsh—the snow at Christmas is not sufficient to incommode them, but sufficient to keep Mr. Elton away from Hartfield.

Where these surroundings fail to please, it is because of the nature of the inhabitants—Jane Fairfax's distress at Donwell, Emma's facetiousness at Box Hill which spoils her enjoyment of the beautiful views.

c. *Background and Theme in 'Persuasion'*

The situation in *Persuasion* is different. Anne is not the vital, energetic heroine that Emma is. She is older, sadder, more experienced—she has lost her first bloom. The novel celebrates her second chance of happiness. But a major concern in the novel is ageing—Sir Walter sees everyone as ageing and losing their looks, and the setting is autumnal, but autumnal with the promise of spring which underlines the theme of the novel.

Anne regrets missing the 'influence so sweet and so sad of the autumnal months in the country' for 'the possible heats of September' in Bath (*P. 5*, 33). During the walk to Winthrop, she finds pleasure in 'the tawny leaves and withered hedges', and the declining year is connected by her with 'declining happiness, and the images of youth and hope, and spring, all gone together'. Yet significantly, the ploughs at work 'spoke the farmer, counteracting the sweets of poetical despondence, and meaning to have spring again' (*10*, 85). The beauty and freshness of Lyme bring a return of beauty to Anne.

But other forms of background enter into the novel—there is the chill, formal glitter of the Elliots and their lodgings in Bath

be contrasted with the warmth and homeliness of the Harville's
ouse at Lyme, the noisy Christmas at Uppercross, and the
qually busy and noisy party they assemble at the White Hart
a Bath. It is against this latter background that Anne's love
tory comes to a happy close with Captain Wentworth's letter,
nd their final meeting is in the streets of Bath, against the busy
ackground of the town:

> And there, as they slowly paced the gradual ascent, heedless
> of every group around them, seeing neither sauntering politicians,
> bustling house-keepers, flirting girls, nor nursery-maids and
> children. . . .'   23, 241

he variety of backgrounds in the novel is closely connected
ith the contrasting themes of the proud aristocracy who have
utlived splendour and usefulness, and the activity and energy
f the new class of gentlemen sailors to whom Anne feels an
astinctive attachment. The last scene, in which we see the lovers
ogether, is placed against the lost world of the Elliots:

> The evening came, the drawing-rooms were lighted up, the
> company assembled. It was but a card-party, it was but a mixture
> of those who had never met before, and those who met too
> often—a common-place business, too numerous for intimacy,
> too small for variety; but Anne had never found an evening
> shorter.   23, 245

. Homes and Characters

he Great Houses, centre of the Jane Austen village community,
re each separately distinguished. To Fanny Price, visiting her
ough-and-tumble family in Portsmouth, Mansfield Park is the
entre of civilised and gracious living. Similarly, Darcy's seat,
'emberley, has the same standing of tradition and graciousness.

> Elizabeth was delighted. She had never seen a place for which
> nature had done more, or where natural beauty had been so
> little counteracted by an awkward taste. . . . The rooms were
> lofty and handsome, and their furniture suitable to the fortune

of their proprietor; but Elizabeth saw, with admiration of his taste, that it was neither gaudy nor uselessly fine; with less of splendor, and more real elegance, than the furniture of Rosings.

PRIDE AND PREJUDICE 43, 245-246

Netherfield, Bingley's rented home, remains suitably un-delineated, and Lady Catherine's Rosings suitably pretentious, and Northanger Abbey ironically modern.

But perhaps more interesting than the way in which these houses are suited to their owners and their place in the story is the way in which they are used to distinguish character. The attitude of a person towards one of the Great Houses is the determinant of their outlook and ambitions. Miss Bingley, Mr. Collins, and Mrs. Elton are all people who make use of the name of the great house, and their acquaintance with it, in order to enhance their own importance. Miss Bingley's 'What a delightful library you have at Pemberley, Mr. Darcy!' and 'Charles, when you build *your* house, I wish it may be half as delightful as Pemberley' are intended as covert compliments to Darcy, and to reveal her own intimacy with his home, and they suggest also her own designs to become the future Mrs. Darcy. Mr. Collins' praise of Rosings indicates his subservience to Lady Catherine as well as his foolishness. Mrs. Elton's exclamations as to the similarity of Hartfield to Maple Grove ('My brother Mr. Suckling's seat'), reveal her vulgarity, and determination to show that she is equal, through her sister, with Emma and Hartfield:

> 'Very like Maple Grove indeed!—She was quite struck by the likeness!—That room was the very shape and size of the morning-room at Maple Grove. . . . And the staircase . . . was . . . placed exactly in the same part of the house. . . . And it is not merely the house—the grounds, I assure you, as far as I could observe, are strikingly like.' EMMA 32, 272-273

Mr. Rushworth, in *Mansfield Park*, reveals his stupidity, his poverty of ideas, and slavish following of the fashion for picturesque landscape gardening in his talk of his own seat, Sotherton, and his friend Smith's place.

Not only Great Houses, but smaller homes also are used by Jane Austen to forward her plot and characterisation. The home of the Prices at Portsmouth is 'the abode of noise, disorder, and impropriety. Nobody was in their right place, nothing was done as it ought to be' (*M.P. 39*, 388-389). And this reflects the character of Fanny's parents. Her father 'was more negligent of his family, his habits were worse, and his manners coarser, than she had been prepared for' (*39*, 389). Her mother 'was a partial, ill-judging parent, a dawdle, a slattern, who neither taught nor restrained her children, whose house was the scene of mis-management from beginning to end . . .' (*39*, 390). By contrast:

> At Mansfield, no sounds of contention, no raised voice, no abrupt bursts, no tread of violence was ever heard; all proceeded in a regular course of cheerful orderliness . . . every body's feelings were consulted. . . . Here, every body was noisy, every voice was loud. . . . Whatever was wanted, was halloo'd for. . . . The doors were in constant banging, the stairs were never at rest, nothing was done without a clatter, nobody sat still, and nobody could command attention when they spoke. *39*, 392

Mansfield is 'elegance, propriety, regularity, harmony', 'peace and tranquility'.

Underlying the description of two contrasting houses here are definite moral standards, and it is of the moral outlook that we are to be aware. Terms such as 'disorder and impropriety' 'ill-judging', 'negligent' are opposed to terms such as 'orderliness', 'propriety', 'harmony'.

But it is not smallness or poverty that, to Jane Austen, makes a house uncomfortable—it is the character of its owners. Thus, the Harvilles' home in *Persuasion* has 'rooms so small as none but those who invite from the heart could think capable of accommodating so many' yet it is 'the picture of repose and domestic happiness' (*11*, 98).

Thus we see that background, although not obtrusive, is nevertheless of great importance in forwarding character, plot, atmosphere, and theme.

10

A Note on Jane Austen's Style

In its rhythm, its sense of order and decorum, Jane Austen's style is eighteenth-century, based on her favourite Dr. Johnson and probably also on the sermons she was fond of reading. It is a style capable of many nuances within a narrow range of devices, and it may be of use to the reader if we examine some of its characteristics here.

GENERALISATIONS

The general truth, beloved of the eighteenth century and expressing either irony or a moral maxim, is frequently found in her work. Johnson's work abounds in such moralisations:

> It has been observed, that they who most loudly clamour for liberty do not most liberally grant it.   LIFE OF JOHN MILTON

> Friendship has no tendency to secure veracity. . . .
>
> LIFE OF POPE

In the novels, generalisations of the lighter kind, often purely comic in intention, frequently appear: 'How quick come the reasons for approving what we like' (*P.*); 'A family of ten children will be always called a fine family, where there are heads and arms and legs enough for the number. . . ' (*N.A.*). Her characters themselves draw generalised conclusions from the behaviour of others. Thus, Emma on Mr. Weston: 'General benevolence, but not general friendship, made a man what he ought to be' (*38*, 320). Sometimes the generalisation is introduced only to be ironically denied:

> Jane had already written a few lines to her sister to announce their safe arrival in London; and when she wrote again, Elizabeth hoped it would be in her power to say something of the Bingleys.

Her impatience for this second letter was *as well rewarded as impatience generally is.* Jane had been a week in town, without either seeing or hearing from Caroline [Bingley]. (my italics)

PRIDE AND PREJUDICE *26*, 147

Thus the solid expectation set up by means of the generalisation is then reversed.

But mostly, such generalisations give the impression of relating to an established and accepted moral code, and are in some degree responsible, therefore, for the sense of stability in moral values and decorum which her work gives: 'The indignities of stupidity, and the disappointment of selfish passion, can excite little pity'; 'Seldom, very seldom, does complete truth belong to any human disclosure; seldom can it happen that something is not a little disguised or a little mistaken. . . '. As in the latter case, her generalisations often appear at a point of intense emotion, and have the effect of distancing and containing the emotion by applying it from the individual character to mankind in general: 'The enthusiasm of a woman's love is even beyond the researches of the fondest biographer.' Elinor 'was oppressed, she was overcome by her own felicity;—and *happily disposed as is the human mind to be easily familiarized with any change for the better,* it required several hours to give sedateness to her spirits, or any degree of tranquility to her heart' (my italics).

THE ABSTRACT

The habit of seeing people and actions through abstract ideas, again an eighteenth-century characteristic, is common in Jane Austen. The quotation from Johnson on p. 150, 'Friendship has no tendency to secure veracity', is an example. The idea of friendship is dealt with, becoming the subject of the sentence, rather than the person who experiences the friendship. In the same way, Jane Austen often has an abstract of some kind— concept, idea, or emotion—taking the place of the actor, thus softening or removing the effects of emotion. Edward Ferrars is removed from the action of loving Lucy Steele—instead, infatuation is blinded by beauty and good nature in the following sentence: 'The youthful infatuation of nineteen would naturally blind him to every thing but her beauty and good nature (*S. & S.* 23, 140). And Mr. Elton's attitude to Emma after his disastrous proposal is similarly extracted from the man into an abstract emotion: 'Resentment could not have been more plainly spoken than in a civility to her father, from which she was so pointedly excluded' (17, 140). The Prices' home at Portsmouth is seen as a home of certain abstract concepts: 'It was the abode of noise, disorder, and impropriety' (*M. P.* 39, 388). And when Anne and Captain Wentworth are eventually to walk together alone, the same abstractions are used to describe outward appearance and inward emotion: 'There could be only a most proper alacrity, a most obliging compliance for public view; and smiles reined in and spirits dancing in private rapture' (*P.* 23, 240).

Similarly, her characters are often described in terms of moral concepts. Anne, 'with an elegance of mind and sweetness of character, which must have placed her high with any people of real understanding, was nobody with either father or sister' (*P.* 1, 5). The description itself is a moral comment of an unobtrusive kind. Edward Ferrars' 'understanding was good, and his education had given it solid improvement'(*S. & S.* 3, 15). To Henry Crawford, Fanny appears to have 'steadiness and regularity of conduct, such a high notion of honour, and such an observance of decorum . . . faith and integrity . . .' (*M. P.* 30, 294).

The use of generalisation and abstract terms gives weight and authority to her style, and also gives support to the moral basis of her world.

BALANCE

We are often struck by the symmetry of her style, and this symmetry rests on her habit of using a rhetorical balance which in turn establishes a sense of logic and order in her work. This balance of style is used for many purposes.

Parallel sentences are frequently introduced to reveal effective and forceful character, and to heighten the confrontation between characters. Mr. Collins proposes marriage to Elizabeth, and Mr. and Mrs. Bennet differ absolutely over Elizabeth's rejection of him. To emphasise this conflict, Jane Austen uses parallel clauses which are identical with the exception of one word or phrase—and of course the emphasis falls on this word or phrase:

> 'Your mother will never see you again if you do *not* marry Mr. Collins, and I will never see you again if you *do*.'
>
> PRIDE AND PREJUDICE 20, 112

The same technique is used to reveal the forcefulness and decisiveness of Elizabeth's character as opposed to Jane's:

> 'It is evident by this . . . that he comes back no more this winter.'
>
> 'It is only evident that Miss Bingley does not mean he *should*.'
>
> PRIDE AND PREJUDICE 21, 117

The balance of ideas which lies at the base of all Jane Austen's work affects her sentence structure by providing a similar balance:

> There, he had learnt to distinguish
>> between
>
> the steadiness of principle and the obstinacy of self-will,
>> between
>
> the darings of heedlessness and the resolution of a collected mind.
>
> PERSUASION 23, 242

The following sentence from Elizabeth Bennet in a similar way demonstrates two possible courses of action, opposite in effect:

> 'You must decide for yourself', said Elizabeth, 'and if upon mature deliberation, you find that
>> the *misery* of disobliging his two sisters
>>> is more than equivalent to
>> the *happiness* of being his wife,
>
> I advise you by all means to refuse him.' (my italics).
>
> PRIDE AND PREJUDICE 21, 119

Decisions are made by balancing one set of conditions against another. To take into account the views of one side only is short-sighted:

> Anne wondered whether it ever occurred to him [Captain Wentworth] now, to question the justness of his own previous opinion as to the universal felicity and advantage of firmness of character; and whether it might not strike him, that, like all other qualities of the mind, it should have its proportions and limits. She thought it could scarcely escape him to feel, that a persuadable temper [by which of course she means herself] might sometimes be as much in favour of happiness, as a very resolute character [Louisa Musgrove].   PERSUASION *12*, 116

The attitudes expressed here by the heroine of *Persuasion* no doubt have the support of the author, and in turn represent the best and most characteristic thought of the eighteenth century. And this method of stating accomplishes a lot without fuss.

> [Mrs. Smith] had . . . two strong claims on her attentions of past kindness and present suffering.   PERSUASION *17*, 152

This is a simple opposition, but it can be developed:

Neither the dissipations
of the past . . .   nor the restrictions of the
                                      present;
neither sickness   nor sorrow
seemed to have closed her heart or ruined her spirits.

PERSUASION *17*, 153

Antithetical ideas, placed together, have this same effect of balance and order:

Her heart was divided between
concern for her sister,   and resentment against all the
                                      others.

PRIDE AND PREJUDICE *24*, 133

Pleased with the preference
of one,   and offended by the neglect of
                                      the other

PRIDE AND PREJUDICE *36*, 208

But sometimes the heartlessness of a passage comes from this desire to seek out antithetical terms:

> ... the Musgroves had had the *ill fortune* of a very troublesome, hopeless son; and the *good fortune* to lose him before he reached his twentieth year. (my italics)   PERSUASION *6*, 50

When Jane Austen works towards a rhetorical climax, she tends to use a particular word which is repeatedly placed at the beginning of successive phrases:

> With the exception, perhaps, of Admiral and Mrs. Croft, who seemed particularly attached and happy, (Anne could allow no other exception even among the married couples) there could have been *no* two hearts *so* open, *no* tastes *so* similar, *no* feelings *so* in unison, *no* countenances *so* beloved. Now they were as strangers.... (my italics)   PERSUASION *8*, 63-64

And in referring once again to the Crofts, Anne says:

> She could have said more on the subject; for she had in fact *so* high an opinion of the Crofts, and considered her father *so* very fortunate in his tenants, felt the parish to be *so* sure of a good example.... (my italics)   *13*, 125

IMAGERY

Jane Austen's imagery is rarely original or striking. In fact her intention seems to be to choose images so conventional that they can be accepted without hesitation by the reader, and so much already part of the language that they go unobserved. Thus we have 'the tumult of her Mind'; 'Such a blow for Harriet'; 'drop a hint'; 'drive away the notion'; 'the fortitude of an angel'; 'she had weathered it'; 'the choicest gift of Heaven'; 'her eye was employed'; 'made herself mistress of its contents'; 'the slave of his designing friends'.

VERBS

Jane Austen's verbs are also responsible for the unruffled impression given by her work. She rarely uses verbs expressing strong physical action, and this is inevitable in writing of a world where strong physical action is at a minimum. But even so, there is a frequent softening of action and emotional response by the use of the passive voice or the impersonal construction. Thus, it is not *Catherine* who is disappointed and distressed by finding the Abbey a modern building but, 'To an imagination which had hoped for the smallest divisions, and the heaviest stone-work, for painted glass, dirt and cobwebs, the difference was very distressing'. 'It vexed her to see him expose himself to such a man.' 'It is not of peculiar, but of general evils, which I am now complaining.' 'If there is no other objection to my marrying your nephew, I shall certainly not be kept from it, by knowing that his mother and aunt wished him to marry Miss De Bourgh.'

THE EXCEPTIONS

But when the occasion demands it, she can use the colloquial term, the unusual image, and the direct statement with an effect which is more remarkable by contrast with the rest of her style. Thus, in *Mansfield Park*, we have the sudden 'trollopy-looking maid-servant' who meets Fanny at her Portsmouth home; and in speech, colloquialisms are used to present character: 'Sharp is the word, you see,' says Mr. Price. In *Emma:* 'their straight-forward emotions left no room for the little zigzags of embarrassment.' And when a record of swift, direct movement is necessary, she can give it: 'A sudden scud of rain driving full in her face, made it impossible for her to observe any thing further . . . and she was actually under the Abbey walls, was springing, with Henry's assistance, from the carriage, was beneath the shelter of the old porch . . .' '. . . Elizabeth continued her walk alone, crossing field after field at a quick pace, jumping over stiles and springing over puddles with impatient activity, and finding herself at last within view of the house, with weary ancles, dirty stockings, and a face glowing with the warmth of exercise.'

The following passage—Mr. Elton's proposal to Emma—contains examples of many of her characteristics of style.

'She was immediately preparing to speak' is used, and not 'She was about to speak.' As a result, the action of speaking is removed further back into the earlier stage of preparation. The passive voice is there—'her subject cut up—her hand seized—her attention demanded'—and linked with the use of abstracts, for it is not Emma, but 'her subject' and 'her attention' which are involved. And there is the use of indirect speech, and moreover at a moment of climax: 'Mr. Elton . . . declaring sentiments which must be already well known, hoping—fearing. . . .' Yet the passage moves quickly and builds to a climax *because of* these effects:

> To restrain him as much as might be, by her own manners, she was immediately preparing to speak with exquisite calmness and gravity of the weather and the night; but scarcely had she begun, scarcely had they passed the sweep-gate and joined the other carriage, than she found her subject cut up—her hand seized—her attention demanded, and Mr. Elton actually making violent love to her: availing himself of the precious opportunity, declaring sentiments which must be already well known, hoping—fearing—adoring. . . .

EMMA *15*, 129

The circumlocutionary beginning is cut into by the repeated passives, and Mr. Elton's indirect and condensed speech only indicates his speed of talking and the conventional manner in which he proposes. It is a fine example of her ability to build up a rhetorical and climactic sentence.

CONCLUSION

Jane Austen was a conscious, if often conventional, stylist, and evidence of this appears throughout her work. The carefully distinguished vulgarities of speech of Lucy and Miss Steele are examples of this, as is Henry Tilney's rather pedantic sermon on the meaning of 'nice'. But to the extent that her effects are deliberately contrived, a careful study of her language enables us to appreciate exactly what she intended since few authors have expressed themselves so precisely.

Bibliography

This is a limited bibliography, designed to bring to the attention of the reader the most easily available and best known of critical and other studies of Jane Austen's novels.

EDITIONS

R. W. Chapman (ed.), *The Novels of Jane Austen*, 6 vols (Oxford Univ. Press, New York, 1923-54). This is the edition referred to in this book. The text is based on collation of the early editions, and contains notes, indexes, and illustrations from contemporary sources. Volume VI, entitled *Minor Works*, contains Jane Austen's juvenilia.
The World's Classics Edition, 6 vols. (Oxford Univ. Press, New York, 1907-31).
All six novels are also available from Modern Library (New York), and William Collins Sons & Co., Ltd. (New York).

LIFE

James E. Austen-Leigh, *Memoir of Jane Austen* (1870), ed. R. W. Chapman (Oxford Univ. Press, New York, 1926).
William and Richard A. Austen-Leigh, *Jane Austen: Her Life and Letters* (Russell & Russell, New York, 1965).
R. W. Chapman, *Jane Austen: Facts and Problems* (Oxford Univ. Press, New York, 1948).
R. W. Chapman (ed.), *Letters* (Oxford Univ. Press, New York, 1952).

CRITICAL WORKS
A. Individual Novels

Arnold Kettle, *An Introduction to the English Novel*, Vol. (Harper & Row, New York) has a controversial chapter on *Emma*.
Lionel Trilling, 'Jane Austen and *Mansfield Park*', *The Pelican Guide to English Literature*, Vol. 5 (Penguin Books, Baltimore, Md.).

2. General

Ioward S. Babb, *Jane Austen's Novels: The Fabric of Dialogue* (Shoe String Press, Hamden, Conn.). A detailed discussion of Jane Austen's use of language and dialogue.

C. M. Forster, 'Jane Austen', *Abinger Harvest* (Harcourt, Brace & World, Inc., New York).

D. W. Harding, 'Jane Austen and Moral Judgment', *The Pelican Guide to English Literature*, Vol. 5, part II.

Iary Lascelles, *Jane Austen and Her Art* (Oxford Univ. Press, New York, 1939).

Robert Liddell, *The Novels of Jane Austen* (Barnes & Noble, New York, 1963).

Iarvin Mudrick, *Jane Austen: Irony as Defense and Discovery* (Univ. of Calif., Berkeley, Calif., 1968).

B. C. Southam, *Jane Austen's Literary Manuscripts: A study of the novelist's development through the surviving papers* (Oxford Univ. Press, New York, 1964).

ylvia Townshend Warner, *Jane Austen* (British Council Pamphlet, 1951).

Virginia Woolf, 'Jane Austen', *The Common Reader* (Penguin Books, Baltimore, Md.).

Andrew Wright, *Jane Austen's Novels: A Study in Structure* (Oxford Univ. Press, New York, 1953).

Index

Main entries are indicated by heavy type.